SPECIAL

THE OPEN MEDIA PAMPHLET SERIES

EDITION

OTHER OPEN MEDIA PAMPHLET SERIES TITLES

THE OPEN MEDIA PAMPHLET SERIES

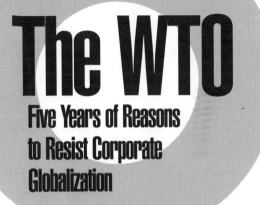

The WTO

Five Years of Reasons to Resist Corporate Globalization

LORI WALLACH and MICHELLE SFORZA
Introduction by Ralph Nader

Series editor Greg Ruggiero

SEVEN STORIES PRESS / NEW YORK

To Michael Francis Dolan, organizer extraordinaire,
for building the international citizens presence in Seattle
to promote the public interest: No New WTO Round,
Turnaround!

Special thanks to Robert Weissman for his invaluable
editorial contribution to this project.

A Seven Stories Press First Edition,
published in association with Open Media.

Open Media Pamphlet Series editor, Greg Ruggiero.

ISBN: 1-58322-035-6

Book design by Cindy LaBreacht

9 8 7 6 5 4 3

Printed in Canada

CONTENTS

INTRODUCTION
By Ralph Nader

In this pamphlet, Public Citizen's Global Trade Watch team comprehensively documents the five-year record of the World Trade Organization (WTO). Unfortunately, the WTO's performance is considerably more damaging than predicted by WTO critics before its approval.

In approving the far-reaching, powerful World Trade Organization and other international trade agreements, such as the North American Free Trade Agreement, the U.S. government, like those of other nations, has ceded much of its flexibility to independently advance health and safety standards that protect citizens. Instead, the U.S. has accepted harsh legal limitations on what domestic policies it may pursue. Approval of these agreements has institutionalized a global economic and political structure that makes every government increasingly hostage to an unaccountable system of transnational governance designed to increase corporate profit, often with complete disregard for social and ecological consequences.

This new governing regime will increasingly provide major generic control over the minute details of the lives of the majority of the world's people. It is not based on the health and economic well-being of people, but rather on the enhancement of the power and wealth of the world's largest corporations and financial institutions.

Under this new system, many decisions affecting people's daily lives are being shifted away from our local and national governments and being placed increasingly in the hands of unelected trade bureaucrats sitting behind closed doors in Geneva, Switzerland. These bureaucrats, for example, are now empowered to dictate whether people in California can pursue certain actions to prevent the destruction of their last virgin forests or determine if carcinogenic pesticides can be banned from their food, or whether the European countries have the right to ban the use of risky biotech materials in their food. Moreover, once the WTO's secret tribunals issue their edicts, no independent appeals are possible. Worldwide conformity or continued payment of fines are required.

At stake is the very basis of democracy and accountable decision-making that is the necessary foundation of any citizen struggle for just distribution of wealth and adequate health, safety, human rights, and environmental protections. An erosion of democratic accountability, and the local, state and national sovereignty that is its embodiment, has taken place over the past several decades.

Multinational companies have shaped the globalization of commerce and finance. The establishment of the WTO marks a landmark formalization and strengthening of their power. In this way, corporate globalization establishes supranational limitations and impinges deeply on the ability of any nation to control commercial activity with democratically enacted laws. Globalization's tactic is to eliminate democratic decision-making and accountability over matters as intimate as the safety of food, pharmaceuticals and motor vehicles, or the way in which a country may use or conserve its land, water, minerals and other resources. What we have now in this type of globalization is a slow motion coup d'etat, a low intensity war waged to redefine free society—democracy and its non-commercial health, safety and other protections—as subordinate to the dictates of international trade—i.e. big business *uber alles*.

One cannot open a newspaper today without reading about myriad examples of the problems that concentrated power spawns: reduced standards of living for most people in the developed and developing world; growing unemployment worldwide; deadly infectious diseases; massive environmental degradation and natural resource shortages; growing political chaos; and a global sense of despair, not hope and optimism, for the future. Conspiratorial meetings have not been necessary to fuel the push for globalization. Many corporate officials share a common, perverse outlook. To them, the globe is viewed primarily as a common market and capital source. Governments, laws and democracy are inconvenient factors that restrict their exploitation and limit their profit. From their perspective, the goal is to eliminate market barriers on a global scale. From any other humane perspective, such barriers are seen as valued safeguards established to protect a nation's population—that is, every nation's laws that foster their economies, their citizens' health and safety, the sustainable use of their land and resources, and so on. In stark contrast, for multinational corporations, the diversity that is a blessing of democracy and that results from diffuse decision-making is itself the major barrier to be bypassed or removed. On rare occasions, promoters of the economic globalization agenda have been frank about their intentions. "Governments should interfere in the conduct of trade as little as possible," said GATT (General Agreement on Tariffs and Trade) Director General Peter Sutherland, in a March 3, 1994, speech in New York City where he promoted U.S. approval of the WTO.

Even more alarming is the definition of "trade" these days which is used increasingly to describe a large portion of each nation's economic and political structures. The WTO and other trade agreements have moved way beyond their traditional roles of setting quotas and tariffs. Now these institute new and unprecedented controls over democratic governance. Erasing national laws and economic boundaries to foster capital mobility and "free trade," a term that ought properly to be called corporate-managed trade (since it produces constraints, not freedom, for the rest of us) has led the likes of American Express, Cargill, General Motors, Monsanto, Union Carbide, Shell, Citigroup, Pfizer and other mega-corporations to rejoice. However, the prospect of global commerce without democratic controls is brewing a disaster for the rest of the world

LORI WALLACH & MICHELLE SFORZA

left uniquely vulnerable to unrestrained corporate activity amid declining living, health and environmental standards.

Economist Herman Daly issued an important warning in his January 1994 "Farewell Lecture to the World Bank." The push to eliminate the nation-state's capacity to regulate commerce, he said, "is to wound fatally the major unit of community capable of carrying out any policies for the common good. ... Cosmopolitan globalism weakens national boundaries and the power of national and subnational communities, while strengthening the relative power of transnational corporations."

The philosophy allegedly behind the globalization agenda is that maximizing global economic deregulation will in itself result in broad economic and social benefits. However, anyone who believes this philosophy or that corporate economic globalization has any underpinnings except maximizing short-term profit, need only consider the case of U.S.-China economic relations. When only human rights were at issue in 1994, the Clinton administration ended the historical linkage between favorable trade status and a country's human rights record. Instead it supported renewal of China's Most Favored Nation (MFN) status. However, in early 1995, when property rights were in question, McDonald's lease and Mickey Mouse's royalties were cause for $1 billion dollars in threatened U.S. trade restrictions against China. This threat resulted in Chinese government policy changes to enforce intellectual property restrictions.

Similarly, economic globalization's primary mechanisms—the WTO and NAFTA—do not target all "fetters" on commerce for elimination. Rather, the agreements promote elimination of restrictions that protect people, while increasing protection for corporate interests. Regulation of commerce for environmental, health or other social goals is strictly limited or challenged. For example, selling products internationally made with child labor is WTO-legal.

Proposals to strengthen obsolete or antiquated standards are chilled from the start by the real prospect of a WTO challenge. This leads to a de facto moratorium on efforts to upgrade and create new standards, i.e., self censorship. Labor rights, which were to be included in the Uruguay Round, were entirely left out as inappropriate limitations on global commerce. But regulation of commerce to protect monopolistic corporate property rights—such as intellectual property—was expanded. The right for capital to be invested in any country in any economic sector without conditions was also strengthened.

By giving up the right to condition investment in a country on certain societal standards, such as not red-lining neighborhoods, or the entry of products into domestic markets in compliance with national rules, countries have damaged whatever leverage they had on corporate behavior. U.S. corporations long ago learned how to pit states against each other in "a race to the bottom" to profit from whatever a state would impose on its citizens the lowest wages, the lowest pollution standards, and the lowest taxes for big business. Often a federal standard would stop such manipulation. Now, through NAFTA and the WTO, multinational corporations can play this game at the global level, pitting country against country. After all, passing off to the public environmental and social costs such as toxic dumping, child labor and dictatorial repression against workers is another way for corporations to boost their profits. Workers, consumers and communities in all countries lose; short-term profits soar and big business "wins."

Under the WTO, not only are the minimum levels of living standards and environmental and health safeguards at risk, but also the very principles and processes of democracy by which such standards are fought for and won. Enactment of these so-called "free trade" deals virtually guarantees that democratic efforts to ensure that corporations pay their fair share of taxes, provide their employees

LORI WALLACH & MICHELLE SFORZA

a decent living standard or limit their pollution of the air, water and land will be met with the refrain: "You can't burden us like that. If you do, we won't be able to compete. We'll have to close down and move to a country that offers us a more hospitable climate." This sort of intimidation is extremely powerful. Communities already devastated by plant closures and a declining manufacturing base are desperate not to lose more jobs. They know all too well that exit threats of this kind are often carried out.

One of the clearest lessons that emerges from a study of industrialized societies is that the centralization of commerce is environmentally and democratically unsound. No one denies the usefulness of having trade between nations. But societies need to focus more attention on fostering community-oriented alternatives. Very often smaller-scale operations are more flexible and adaptable to local needs and environmentally sustainable production methods. These are also more susceptible to democratic control. Their officers are far less likely to threaten to migrate and more likely to perceive their interests as more overlapping with community interests. Similarly, allocating power to lower-level governmental bodies tends to increase citizen power. Concentrating power in distant international organizations, as the trade pacts do, tends to remove critical decision-making from citizen control. You can talk to your city council representative but not some faceless international trade bureaucrat at the WTO in Geneva. If local or state decisions can be jeopardized by a foreign country's mere charge that their standards are a "non-tariff trade barrier," if a country must pay a tribute in trade sanctions to maintain laws ruled to be trade barriers by closed and autocratic foreign tribunals, if a company's claim that the burden that important citizen safeguards would impose causes them to pick up their stakes and move abroad, then standards of living and the all-important underlying standards of justice worldwide will continue to spiral downward. This is what happens when democratic values are subjugated to the imperatives of international trade.

Following the establishment of the WTO, the corporate globalization process and its effects are continuing to exacerbate stagnant economic conditions for most of the world's people. In the U.S., if we do not make the connection between our local problems and the corporate drive for economic and political control, then others will be blamed for these unavoidable and increasing problems. "It's the immigrants!" "It's the welfare system!" "It's greedy farmers or workers!" "It's the regulatory agencies!" "It's the tort system!" Allowing such camouflage of the real causes of society's multifaceted problems means a massive diversion of our focus, dividing people against each other to the benefit of the agenda of mega-corporations.

Thus, what we face now is a race against time: How can citizens most effectively mobilize a reversal of the expanding globalization agenda while they defend our democratic spaces, instincts and institutions from assault? The degree of suppression and subterfuge necessary to continue along the downward path will be hard to maintain in the presence of any vigorous democratic oversight. However, actually reversing NAFTA, the WTO and the push toward globalization will require a revitalized citizen democracy in the United States and movement building across national borders. Replacing the WTO-GATT with a pull-up, not a pull-down, system of global commerce is the goal. The purpose of this pamphlet is to inform citizens about the WTO's five year track record, and to encourage the pursuit of creative democratic alternatives, at every level, to corporate globalization.

I. THE WTO'S SLOW-MOTION
COUP D'ETAT OVER DEMOCRATIC SOCIETY

The World Trade Organization is carrying out a slow-motion coup d'etat over democratic governance worldwide.

Unlike past trade pacts, the WTO (World Trade Organization) and its underlying agreements move far beyond traditional commercial matters such as tariffs, import quotas or requirements that foreign and domestic goods be treated equally. The WTO's provisions set limits on the strength of countries' food safety laws and the comprehensiveness of product labeling policies. They forbid countries from banning products made with child labor. They can even regulate expenditure of local tax dollars (for instance, prohibiting environmental or human rights considerations in government purchasing decisions).

The WTO, established on January 1, 1995, as part of the Uruguay Round Agreements of the General Agreement on Tariffs and Trade (GATT) and now with 134 Member countries, has rapidly accumulated a sordid record. Binding decisions from its enforcement tribunals have undermined consumer and environmental protections around the world. And corporations have used the threat of WTO action to roll back, block or chill countless rules designed to benefit workers, consumers and the environment, and to promote human rights and development in the world's poor countries.

This unfortunate outcome could have been predicted. Indeed, it was. When the Uruguay Round was being negotiated, environmental, labor and consumer groups warned that the GATT system, which had existed for decades, was being dramatically recast and expanded in a way that would subjugate core public interest needs—such as accountable governance, environmental protection, health and safety, and human and labor rights—to corporate interests.

Proponents of the Uruguay Round and the WTO dismissed these concerns as ill-informed doomsday prophesies. They promised that the Uruguay Round and the WTO would pose no threat to domestic sovereignty or democratic, accountable policymaking. They also promised enormous economic gains worldwide if the Uruguay Round were implemented: The U.S. trade deficit would decrease by $60 billion in ten years.[1] Latin American countries would boom and Asian growth would keep pace. Then-U.S. Treasury Secretary Lloyd Bentsen even predicted that passage of the Uruguay Round would result in an additional $1,700 in annual median income per U.S. family.[2]

Now, nearly five years later, it is clear that the promised economic gains have not materialized. Not only has the WTO failed to live up to its proponents' promises, but it is wreaking continuing damage to health, human rights, safety and environmental safeguards.

This pamphlet, an abridged version of a longer (and much more heavily footnoted) book called *Whose Trade Organization?; Corporate Globalization and the Erosion of Democracy* surveys the actual outcomes of nearly five years of WTO operations.

Our purpose here is to document an insidious shift in decision-making away from democratic, accountable fora—where citizens have a chance to fight for the public interest—to distant, secretive and unaccountable international bodies, whose rules and operations are dominated by corporate interests. Ironically, the U.S., with some of the world's most open, accountable policymaking procedures, is a leader in using the WTO to undercut democratic institutions and mechanisms around the world.

The full magnitude of this new global governance system is yet to be seen because some WTO rules have not taken full effect. But it is clear that the WTO rules have little to do with the 19th century "free trade" philosophies of Adam Smith or David Ricardo. Rather, the rules create a model of corporate economic globalization that would be most accurately dubbed "corporate managed trade."

Now is the time to ask: Whose trade organization is it? It does not appear to belong to or benefit the majority of the world's citizens. The emerging system favors huge multinational companies and the wealthiest few in developed and developing countries.

But permanent entrenchment of this still-emerging system is not a foregone conclusion. Despite the public relations efforts of those who benefit from this arrangement to convince us otherwise, the WTO setup is merely one design; it is not inevitable like the moon's pull on the tides or some other force of nature. Putting into place the WTO and the globalization it implements required its proponents to undertake an enormous amount of planning, public relations and political work. We still have the freedom to oppose the WTO's design, and we still have the power to pursue and develop real alternatives. In other parts of the world, especially in indigenous communities that lack basic resources and access to media, such opportunities do not exist.

If after reading this pamphlet you agree with us that the WTO's outcomes are undesirable and unacceptable, consider ways to act. Working together, communities around the world can create the demand to replace the WTO model with a far more equitable, environmentally sustainable and democratically accountable system.

Promised Economic Gains Fail to Materialize. The long-term social and ecological consequences of the Uruguay Round cannot be known until its terms have been fully implemented. But the economic trends that have emerged so far indicate serious problems. These trends would have to abruptly reverse course merely to return the developing world to better, pre-Uruguay Round conditions, much less to fulfill many of the outlandish predictions of broad benefits served up by Uruguay Round PR spin.

What we do know today is that since the WTO was created, the world has been buffeted by unprecedented financial instability. Economic growth in the developing world has slowed. Income inequality is rising rapidly between and within countries.[3] Despite productivity gains, wages in many countries have failed to rise.[4] Commodity prices are at all-time lows, causing the standard of living for many people to slide, particularly in Asia, Latin America and Africa.[5] Indeed, in most countries the period under the Uruguay Round has brought dramatic reversals in fortune.

Latin America is foundering, mired in its deepest economic slump since the debt crisis of the 1980s.[6]

East Asia is paralyzed by an economic crisis caused in part by the very investment and financial service sector deregulation that WTO rules intensify and spread to other nations. While the U.S. media have announced that the crisis is over, people living in South Korea know better. There, the crisis has quadrupled unemployment and precipitated a 200% increase in absolute poverty, effectively rolling back decades of economic progress.[7]

Global economic indicators generally paint a tragic picture: The income gap between the fifth of the world's people living in the richest countries and the fifth in the poorest was 74-to-1 in 1997, up from 60-to-1 in 1990 and 30-to-1 in 1960.[8] By 1997, the richest 20% captured 86% of world income, with the poorest 20% capturing a mere 1%.[9]

In the U.S., the trade deficit is at an all-time high, $218 billion and climbing,[10] having ballooned—not declined as promised—from $98 billion in 1994. The median family income has not risen by $1,700 per year during any of the past four years as the Clinton administration promised.[11]

While the economic numbers paint a telling picture, they are but one part of the story. Of equal importance, but less well known, is the WTO's consistent record of eroding public interest policies designed to safeguard the environment, our communities' health and safety, human rights and democracy.

WTO Challenges and Threats Undermine the Public Interest. The expansive Uruguay Round Agreements' constraints on the ability of governments to maintain public interest regulations are enforced through a freestanding WTO tribunal system empowered to judge countries' laws for WTO-compliance.

Since it was created in 1995, one out of four WTO challenges has involved an environmental, health or safety policy. In each instance the WTO has ruled such policies to be illegal trade barrier that must be eliminated or changed. Nations whose laws were declared trade barriers by the WTO—or that were merely threatened with prospective WTO action—have eliminated or watered down policies to meet WTO requirements. In addition to undermining important policies, this trend has a chilling effect on countries' inclinations to initiate new environmental, human rights or safety laws because they want to avoid WTO challenges.

The very mechanics of the WTO, which are skewed in favor of corporations and trade, pre-ordain this outcome. WTO business is conducted by committees and panels that meet behind closed doors in Geneva, Switzerland. In sharp contrast to U.S. domestic courts and even other international arbitration systems, there is a startling lack or "transparency"—public disclosure and accountability. This leads to overwhelming concentrations of corporate power and influence.

The string of public interest laws ruled against and developing countries are among the biggest losers in this system. Developing countries generally do not have the money and expertise either to bring cases to the WTO or defend themselves before the WTO. Many simply capitulate to corporate threats and amend their laws before the matter even reaches the WTO.

Because the WTO is still so young, the cases described in this pamphlet are merely the beginning, offering a frightening glimpse of what is still to come unless significant changes are made.

The primary problem stems from the fact that countries' domestic policy goals and laws must pass muster with the WTO, which, among other constraints, requires that laws and regulations implementing even WTO-permitted goals prove to be least trade restrictive.

Further, WTO rules prohibit countries from treating physically similar products differently based on how they are made or harvested. For instance, in the eyes of the WTO, tuna caught in dolphin-safe nets can be treated no differently than tuna caught in nets that ensnare dolphins. This is why the Clinton administration worked with some of the Congress' leading anti-environmental members to water down a popular U.S. law designed to prevent dolphins from being killed in tuna nets which was ruled to be a trade violation. This backwards logic also jeopardizes laws banning trade in goods made with child labor or trade with countries where human rights abuses take place.

WTO philosophies also undermine global cooperation on the environment, health and human rights. If a country is a WTO member, its domestic implementation of other international commitments must comply with WTO rules. For instance, the WTO ruled against provisions of the U.S. Endangered Species Act that required shrimpers to protect endangered sea turtles—a law that implemented U.S. commitments under the global environmental treaty called Convention on Trade in Endangered Species (CITES). Now, the U.S. and EU are threatening Japan's attempt to enact laws to implement the Kyoto Treaty on global climate change as WTO-illegal.

WTO rules set a ceiling on safety by making certain international standards the only presumptively WTO-legal standards. Domestic standards on health, the environment and public safety that are higher than international ones must pass a set of stringent tests in order *not* to be considered trade barriers. Meanwhile, there is no floor on health or safety that all countries must meet; there is no requirement that international standards be met, only that they cannot be exceeded.

The cases also clearly show that the WTO system effectively turns the very premise by which some progressive governments have handled environmental, food safety and other human health-related policies on its head. Generally, manufacturers are required to prove that a product is safe before it can be sold, and countries do not permit the product to enter the marketplace until the company has submitted the proof. Under WTO rules, however, the burden is completely reversed. Governments must prove that a product is unsafe before they ban it and must clear near-impossible procedural and evidentiary hurdles to do so.

With the establishment of the WTO, judgements over such key areas as food safety have been pulled from the hands of domestic legislatures and effectively ceded to the international corporate interests that helped write the WTO rules. Following an adverse WTO ruling, Europe must now absorb $115 million annually in WTO-authorized trade sanctions to maintain a ban on beef containing residues of artificial growth hormones.

Another alarming aspect of this new WTO system is the fact that *nations* are serving as corporations' servants, agreeing to challenge laws that the corporations oppose. The U.S. went to bat for Chiquita, the banana giant, when it successfully attacked Europe's preferential treatment of bananas from former EU colonies in the Caribbean.[12] The U.S. does not produce bananas for export and most of Chiquita's employees are underpaid farm workers laboring on its vast Central American plantations.[13] The EU has announced that it has no choice but to rescind its preferential treatment, an action that could have a devastating impact on the small, independent banana farmers in the Caribbean.

Often, the mere threat of a challenge suffices. For

instance, after the U.S. threatened WTO action, South Korea weakened two food safety laws—one pertaining to the shelf life for meat, the other dealing with fruit and vegetable inspections.

Because developing countries generally lack the resources and expertise to defend challenges, threats to the policies can be particularly devastating. However, developing countries haven't been the only losers. Rich countries have seen some of their valuable policies gutted too. The threats of WTO action described in this pamphlet are merely the tip of the iceberg, given that so much of the activity is shrouded in secrecy.

WTO Trend: Commerce Always Takes Precedence. The overall theme that emerges from reviewing the WTO's record: In the WTO forum, global commerce takes precedence over everything—democracy, public health, equity, the environment, food safety and more. Indeed, under WTO rules, global commerce takes precedence over even small business.

The WTO's manic tilt toward commercial values is perhaps best highlighted by its rules seeking to commodify everything—to turn everything into a form of property—so that it can be bought and sold. For instance, the new system gives patents—and thus exclusive marketing rights—for life forms and indigenous knowledge. Consider what has happened in India, where the indigenous population has used the neem tree for medicinal purposes for generations. After a U.S. importer discovered the tree's pharmaceutical properties, multinational companies from the U.S. and Japan sought and received numerous patents on products made from the tree, leaving the indigenous populations unable to profit from knowledge they have developed over centuries.

Consider, too, the plight of subsistence farmers. Under the WTO's new intellectual property guarantees, a company can obtain ownership rights—literally a patent—over the knowledge and effort of the local farmers who bred an adapted seed over generations. Once a company holds the patent for a particular seed variety, it can force cashless farmers either to pay an annual royalty, buy new seeds each year or no longer use the variety, which may be the only one available or effective in that region.

The WTO's Unprecedented Dispute Resolution System. How are such extreme rules enforced against countries around the world? The WTO contains the strongest enforcement procedures of any international agreement now in force. The WTO is a free-standing organization with "legal personality" (the same political status of the United Nations) and with self-executing enforcement, meaning that the WTO contains binding dispute mechanisms to enforce its trade rules. Countries in the WTO are called "Members," are bound to all WTO terms, and can stave off a WTO enforcement action only if *all* other WTO Members unanimously agree.

Unlike the GATT before it, WTO panel rulings are automatically binding and do not require unanimous consent to be adopted. Nor do WTO trade sanctions need consensus approval. Indeed, the WTO is unique among all other international agreements in that consensus is required to *stop* action. Once a WTO tribunal has declared a country's law WTO-illegal, the country must change its law or face trade sanctions. Even more alarming, it is the official position of the U.S. government that such sanctions or negotiated compensation are only interim measures and that WTO rules require countries to amend their domestic laws.[14]

The WTO's binding dispute resolution procedure and the Uruguay Round's expansive new rules encroaching into areas traditionally considered the realm of domestic policy effectively shift many decisions regarding public health and safety, environmental and social concerns from democratically elected domestic bodies to WTO tribunals meeting behind closed doors in Geneva, Switzerland.

After almost five years of WTO panel rulings, the record

is clear: countries that can afford to launch WTO challenges generally are winning. To date, WTO tribunals have almost always sided with a challenging country and ruled against the targeted law. In only three out of 22 completed WTO cases did the respondents win. As of July 1999, the U.S. had lost every completed case brought against it, with the WTO labeling as illegal U.S. policies ranging from sea turtle protection and clean air regulations to anti-dumping duties.[15] The U.S.—which has brought more complaints than any other country—was a claimant or co-claimant in nine of the 22 cases.[16]

No democratically achieved environmental, health, food safety or environmental law challenged at the WTO has survived the attack. All have been declared barriers to trade.

WTO Tribunals: Secret Proceedings, Lack of Due Process. Challenges by WTO member countries to other countries' laws are heard by tribunals sitting at the WTO's Geneva Headquarters and governed by the Uruguay Round Dispute Resolution Understanding (DSU). The DSU provides only one specific operating rule—that all panel activities and documents are confidential.[17] Under this WTO rule, dispute panels operate in secret, documents are restricted to the countries in the dispute, due process and citizen participation are absent and no outside appeal is available. The WTO's lower panel and Appellate Body meet in closed sessions and the proceedings are confidential. All documents are also kept confidential unless a government voluntarily releases its own submissions to the public.[18] The closed nature of the dispute process prevents domestic proponents of health, environmental or other policies that are being challenged from obtaining sufficient information about the proceedings to provide input.

WTO disputes are heard by tribunals composed of three panelists. The WTO secretariat nominates panel members for each dispute, and the disputing parties may oppose nominations only for "compelling reasons."[19] The only recourse after a panel ruling is to appeal to the WTO Appellate Body. To date, the Appellate Body, whose panelists are paid WTO employees, have reversed only one case.

Bureaucrats with Trade Expertise Judge Environmental, Public Health, Worker Rights and Economic Development Policies. Qualifications for serving on WTO dispute panels include past service on GATT panels, past representation of a country before a trade institution or tribunal, past service as a senior trade policy official of a WTO Member country, and teaching experience in or publishing on international trade law or policy.[20] These qualifications promote the selection of panelists with a stake in the existing trade system and rules. They also winnow out potential panelists who do not share an institutionally derived philosophy about international commerce and the role of the GATT system that supports the status quo.

There are no mechanisms for ensuring that individuals serving as panelists have any expertise in the subject of the dispute before them. This is particularly worrisome in disputes concerning health and environmental measures, as the WTO's rules do not even require panelists to consult with experts.

Conflict of Interest Standards at the WTO: "Don't Ask, Don't Tell." As established in the Uruguay Round Agreements, the WTO dispute resolution system lacked any mechanism guaranteeing that panelists do not have potential conflicts of interest in serving on a panel. Rules of Conduct adopted in 1996 rely on voluntary disclosure of conflicts and voluntary withdrawal from panels—standards so weak that they are pointless.[21] This was made clear in a case where an International Chamber of Commerce representative who also serves on the board of Nestlé was appointed to judge the WTO challenge of the Helms-Burton sanctions against certain foreign investors in Cuba, where Nestlé has a plant. [22]

Adding Insult to Injury: WTO Limits Citizens' Ability to Rectify Panel's Shortcomings. The lack of competence on health, environment and other matters among tribunal members could have been rectified to some extent by requiring the participation by *ad hoc* independent experts on panels or by requiring panels to consider third-party submissions from parties with a demonstrated interest in the case (*amici curiae* or *amicus* briefs). The WTO's dispute resolution system does neither.

WTO panels are allowed, but not required, to seek information and technical advice from outside individuals and expert bodies. However, the names of such experts are kept secret until the panel issues its report on the case,[23] making it impossible to prevent conflicts of interest among the technical experts.

Even though the WTO recently lifted its absolute ban on *amicus* briefs, interested parties who wish to provide input in the form of *amicus* briefs face an array of obstacles, including winning the agreement of their government to include the brief in the official submission—a difficult challenge indeed for public interest groups and others that may disagree with their government's position—but the only way to submit a brief.[24]

Winner Takes All: No Outside Appeal Allowed, Cross-Sectoral Sanctions Permitted. WTO panels establish specific deadlines by which a losing country must implement the panel's decision to change or eliminate a policy.[25] If this deadline is not met, the winning party may request negotiations to determine mutually acceptable compensation.[26] If compensation is not sought or not agreed to, the winning party may request WTO authorization to impose trade sanctions.[27] Once requested, sanctions can be stopped only if there is unanimous consensus of all WTO Members against sanctions, requiring the winning country to also agree to drop its sanctions request.[28] This unique WTO design is precisely opposite of the sovereignty protections found in most international agreements where consensus is required to move forward.

And unlike GATT, WTO sanctions may be applied "cross-sectorally," meaning that a country can retaliate against the key exports of the noncompliant party and not simply against similar products in the same sector.[29] This places an especially large burden on developing countries that have not diversified their exports and could thus be more easily pressured by threats of retaliation from a developed country against a single major export.

For a government that loses a case, there is no appeals process outside of the WTO's Appellate Body. The DSU merely provides that those persons serving on the Appellate Body are to be "persons of recognized authority with demonstrated expertise in law, international trade and the subject matter of the covered Agreements generally."[30] Again, there are no provisions for environmental, consumer law or labor experts to serve on the panel. Unlike members of lower panels who are called to serve in particular cases, the appeal panelists are part of a seven-person standing WTO body, meaning that they are on the permanent WTO payroll.[31] This is a startling conflict in its own right, given that every case requires a determination of whether domestic law or the Appellate Body tribunalists' employer's rules take precedence.

The Seattle WTO Ministerial Meeting. In late November 1999, the 134 countries that are WTO Members were to meet in Seattle, Washington, for a Ministerial Summit to determine the future work plan of the WTO. Most corporate interests sought a major expansion of WTO rules to cover education and health services and to establish new rights for currency speculators and foreign investors (bringing into the WTO the Multilateral Agreement on Investment, a controversial proposed treaty killed by broad public and legislative opposition in 1998).

The U.S. scaled back its already modest agenda for labor

or environmental safeguards at the WTO and instead is focused on obtaining an agreement at the Ministerial to:

➤ launch new negotiations to expand the scope of the WTO to include new service sectors, such as health and education;

➤ expand the rules concerning government procurement to all WTO countries, first by requiring all WTO Member countries to publicly list all of their procurement activity and to agree to future negotiations limiting the ability of governments to take non-commercial considerations (such as environmental protection or economic development) into account when making purchasing decisions;

➤ sign a "Global Free Logging" pact that could increase deforestation by 4% per year;

➤ launch new negotiations on WTO protections for biotechnology products (such as genetically modified organisms); and

➤ further deregulate agricultural trade.

Much of the U.S. government's plan to expand the current WTO model runs contrary to U.S. public opinion and would undermine the ability of citizens to participate in making key decisions affecting their lives. A recent survey showed that 81 percent of Americans believe Congress should oppose trade pacts that give one nation the power to overturn consumer safety, labor or environmental laws in another.

A global coalition of citizens groups—consumer, religious, environmental, labor, family farm and others—is calling for a "turnaround" to replace the WTO's damaging provisions. "No New Round, Turnaround" is the rallying cry issued by this large coalition of nongovernmental organizations worldwide.

These concerned groups seek an objective review of the performance under the current WTO rules, with an eye toward scaling back areas that inappropriately invade domestic policymaking, removing some issues from WTO jurisdiction altogether and replacing other WTO rules with versions aimed at serving the broad public interest.

II. THE WTO AND THE ENVIRONMENT

The WTO has been a disaster for the environment. Threats—often by industry but with government support—of WTO-illegality are being used to chill environmental innovation and to undermine multilateral environmental agreements. Already WTO threats and challenges have undermined or threatened to interfere with U.S. Clean Air rules, the U.S. Endangered Species Act, Japan's Kyoto (global warming) Treaty implementation, a European toxics and recycling law, U.S. longhorned beetle infestation policy, EU eco-labels, U.S. dolphin protection legislation and an EU humane trapping law.

Things stand only to get worse, as industry begins to engineer challenges to environmental laws based on the new, stronger anti-environmental provisions developed through the Uruguay Round. A major shift occurred with establishment of the WTO's new rules. Instead of only requiring that domestic and foreign goods be treated equally, the WTO makes value judgements about the *level* of environmental protection or the sorts of policy goals WTO Members pursue.

Strong Enforcement of Anti-Environmental Rules. The Uruguay Round Agreements added a vast array of new anti-environment, anti-conservation provisions to the existing GATT rules, which themselves had drawn fire from environmentalists. These new rules subject a wider array of hard-won environmental laws to scrutiny as so-called "non-tariff barriers" to trade. ("Non-tariff barrier" is jargon for any law or policy that is not a tariff but affects trade.)

The WTO Agreement on Sanitary and Phytosanitary Measures (SPS) explicitly restricts the actions that governments can take relating to food and agriculture policy, including laws to protect food safety or to protect the environment, human, plant or animal health. As a result, many policies that governments use to avoid or contain invasive species infestations from undermining biodiversity can run afoul of WTO's rules. The WTO Agreement on Technical Barriers to Trade (TBT) requires that product standards—a nation's rules governing the contents and characteristics of products—be made as least trade restrictive as possible and, with extraordinarily limited exceptions, be based on international standards. The WTO Agreement on Government Procurement requires that governments take into account only "commercial considerations" when making purchasing decisions. The Agreement on Trade Related Aspects of Intellectual Property (TRIPs) requires that WTO Members provide property rights protection to genetically modified plant varieties even though their long-term environmental impacts have not been established. All of these agreements are enforceable, by threat of sanction, through the WTO's dispute resolution system.

While the WTO publicly states its support for the principles of sustainable development in the WTO ("the [environment] has been given and will continue to be given a high profile on the WTO agenda"),[1] the track record suggests an altogether different set of priorities. Indeed, in a revealing attack of candor, then-WTO Secretary General Renato Ruggiero stated that environmental standards in the WTO are "doomed to fail and could only damage the global trading system."[2]

WTO's New Binding Rules Have Weakened Environmental Safeguards.

CASE 1: U.S. WEAKENS CLEAN AIR RULE TO IMPLEMENT WTO ORDER

The WTO had been in operation only for several months when the first attack on an important environmental law was launched. In response to a challenge initiated by Venezuela and Brazil, a WTO dispute panel in January 1996 ruled that U.S. Clean Air Act regulations adopted under 1990 amendments to the Act were in violation of WTO rules.[3] The U.S. was instructed by the WTO to amend its gasoline cleanliness regulations,[4] which it did by adopting a policy toward limiting contaminants in gasoline that the U.S. Environmental Protection Agency (EPA) earlier had rejected as effectively unenforceable.[5]

In 1994, the EPA had issued a rule implementing Congress' 1990 Clean Air Act amendments requiring reduction of gasoline contaminants. The rule required the cleanliness of gasoline sold in the most polluted cities in the U.S. to improve by 15% over 1990 levels, and all gasoline sold elsewhere in the U.S. to maintain levels of cleanliness at least equal to 1990 levels.

For gasoline producers for which the EPA had documentation of 1990 gasoline cleanliness levels, the EPA set improvement targets based on refineries' actual performance. Gasoline from foreign refiners that sold less than 80% of their gasoline in the U.S. (and thus who were not required to file with EPA) and from domestic refiners without documentation had to match the average actual 1990 contaminant level of all gas refiners able to provide full documentation.

Venezuela and Brazil claimed that the EPA rule could put their gasoline industries at an unfair disadvantage. Even though they were required only to meet average cleanliness levels, they complained that the ostensibly neutral U.S. law could result in some U.S. refineries being permitted to sell gas that was less clean than average while they could not.

The WTO panel sided with Venezuela and Brazil's oil industries. A final 1996 ruling from the WTO Appellate Body held that the U.S. government-set gasoline cleanliness requirements could have a discriminatory *impact* against foreign gasoline.[6]

In August 1997, the EPA replaced the regulation the WTO had proclaimed to be an illegal trade barrier with a new one that was "consistent with the obligations of the

United States under the World Trade Organization"[7] to implement the WTO ruling. The new WTO-consistent rules are identical to an industry proposal that the EPA had previously contended was unenforceable and too costly.[8]

The gasoline case inspired a run of successful challenges against hard-won environmental and public health laws. To date, all GATT/WTO rulings on environmental laws have led (or will lead, if implemented) to the weakening of the measures in question.

CASE 2: CLINTON ADMINISTRATION GUTS DOLPHIN PROTECTION

Under amendments to the U.S. Marine Mammal Protection Act (MMPA), the sale by domestic or foreign fishers of tuna caught with mile-long encirclement nets, known as "purse seine" nets, was banned in the U.S. in 1988. Because schools of tuna in the Eastern Tropical Pacific congregate under schools of dolphins, use of the nets killed millions of dolphins in the that region.[9] Over 30 years, seven million dolphins were drowned, crushed or otherwise killed as a result of purse seine tuna fishing.[10]

In 1991, a GATT panel ruled against Section 101(a)(2) of the U.S. MMPA[11]—which excluded from the U.S. market tuna caught by domestic or foreign fishers using purse seines. The panel interpreted language in GATT's Article III, which prohibits discrimination between products on the basis of *where* they are produced to also forbid distinguishing between products based on *how* they are produced. In 1994, a GATT panel again ruled against the MMPA, this time in response to a similar European challenge.[12]

That the embargo was applied to both the domestic and foreign tuna industries was held irrelevant by the GATT. The first panel found that the law was not "necessary" to protect dolphin health because, in the panel's opinion, the U.S. could have attempted to protect dolphins through other measures that would not have violated GATT.

LORI WALLACH & MICHELLE SFORZA

Given that the rulings against the U.S. dolphin-safe law were issued by GATT—and not WTO—panels, they were not automatically enforceable. Indeed, Mexico and the U.S. agreed not to enforce the ruling because they feared it would undermine passage of the North American Free Trade Agreement (NAFTA).

However, by 1995, with NAFTA passed and the WTO in operation, Mexico demanded that the GATT ruling be enforced. With President Clinton anxious to avoid the public spectacle of a dolphin protection law being eviscerated by the WTO, he sent a letter to Mexican President Ernesto Zedillo declaring that the weakening of the standard "is a top priority for my Administration and for me personally."[13] By 1997, over the opposition of the Marine Mammal Protection Act's original congressional champions and a coalition of environmental, consumer and other public interest groups, Clinton succeeded in implementing the GATT order and thus in gutting the law.

By the fall of 1999—for the first time in over a decade—tuna caught with purse seines will be back on the U.S. market.

The precedent set in the GATT panel's ruling has serious widespread implications. It forbids countries from distinguishing among different *production methods* even if this is done to further a legitimate social or environmental goal. For example, under such reasoning, prohibiting the use of fur harvested by clubbing of harp seals could be GATT-illegal. Similarly, policies banning products involving child labor or even slave labor could be prohibited by the WTO.

Then in 1998, a WTO panel ruled against provisions of the U.S. Endangered Species Act allowing sale of shrimp in the U.S. only if the shrimp are caught in nets equipped with turtle excluder devices.[14] This law applied to U.S. and foreign fishers and implemented U.S. obligations under the global environmental treaty called CITES (Convention on International Trade in Endangered Species)

What's Next? Special Interests Threaten WTO Action to Thwart Environmental Initiatives. The new Uruguay Round texts, such as the Agreement on Technical Barriers to Trade (TBT), formalize the WTO prohibition on rules limiting corporations' market access based on how they produce or process a good—even when the standard is applied equally to domestic and foreign producers.

The TBT Agreement outlines the procedures WTO Members must follow when promulgating product standards or other technical regulations. Its provisions apply to all products, including industrial and agricultural products, but not to health-related food rules or agricultural product regulations dealing with plant pests or animal health. The TBT Agreement limits how governments can regulate trade in the interest of environmental protection by requiring that regulations not be more trade restrictive than is necessary[15] and not differ from international standards.[16]

Although the TBT Agreement has not yet been the subject of a WTO panel ruling, its provisions have already been used by the U.S. to pressure Japan to weaken clean air laws designed to comply with internationally agreed upon targets for CO_2 reduction and to attack an EU prohibition on leg traps deemed cruel to animals. The U.S. government also has argued that labeling products as environmentally friendly to raise environmental awareness among consumers—called eco-labeling—is a technical regulation that should be subject to WTO scrutiny. Canada also has used the TBT Agreement to file a WTO challenge to France's ban on asbestos.[17]

THREAT 1: U.S. PRESSURES EU TO ABANDON HIGH STANDARDS FOR CURTAILING ELECTRONICS INDUSTRY POLLUTION

In what is an important test case, the American Electronics Association (AEA)—with 3,000 member companies, including Motorola and Intel—used the WTO to attack a proposed EU directive to control electronics industry pollution. The AEA claims the EU directive is WTO-illegal because it restricts trade in certain heavy metals used to make electronics products, is not based on an international standard, and is more trade restrictive than necessary to satisfy its objective.[18] A U.S. State Department *demarche* to the EU suggested that the directive runs afoul of WTO rules and urged the EU to adopt the less-stringent U.S. standard for electronics pollution.[19]

The EU directive was designed to minimize waste caused by electronic products and to shift the cost of subsequent environmental cleanup from the public to the electronics industry and is considered state-of-the-art by environmental groups.[20] It requires electronic companies to take responsibility for their products from the cradle to the grave, and is considered state of the art by environmental groups.

First, the directive would ban electronic products containing lead, mercury, cadmium, hexavalent chromium and halogenated flame retardants by the year 2004.[21] The AEA says there is no scientific basis for such a regulation.

Second, it would impose a 5% recycled content rule for plastic electronic components. Third, electronics manufacturers would be made responsible for the recovery and disposal of electronic equipment. But according to the AEA, the EU cannot impose recycling requirements on foreign producers because under WTO rules, the EU has no interest, or right, to advance environmental protection in the foreign country in which the components are made.[22] However, given that these products will eventually be disposed in the EU, the EU reasonably claims to have a significant interest in regulating their content.

In the summer of 1999, the EU proposed to revise the directive, eliminating key provisions on recycling and reversing the bans on some hazardous substances.[23]

This case is a perfect illustration of how WTO rules empower industry and the trade ministries that represent them to chill progress on improved environmental standards. As governments struggle to address environmental hazards, industries in producing nations will issue WTO threats designed to deter action. The regulating countries face a choice between protecting their population or facing WTO dispute panels and the possibility of sanctions.

Threat 2: U.S., EU Auto Industries Attack Japanese Clean Air Rules Implementing Kyoto Treaty

The Japanese government committed itself in the Kyoto Protocol (the global warming treaty) to cut greenhouse gases by 6% from 1990 levels.[24] Japan then launched a comprehensive plan to cut CO_2 emissions that included setting new standards for automobile fuel efficiency, particularly cars in the medium weight category, where the standards had been relatively less rigorous.[25] The Japanese law requires emissions levels equal to those achieved by the most non-polluting engine existing in the middle range weight class. The most non-polluting engine now existing in the class is designed by Mitsubishi.[26]

In 1999, the EU cried foul, shooting off a letter to the WTO TBT Secretariat complaining about the new rules.[27] The U.S. followed suit on behalf of Daimler-Chrysler and the Ford Motor Company.[28] In a March 8, 1999 letter to the Japanese Ministry of Foreign Affairs, the U.S. voiced its support for the objective of reducing CO_2 emissions, while claiming that Japan's new rules may be WTO-illegal.[29] Both the U.S. and the EU question Japan's basing of the new standard on the performance of the Mitsubishi engine; citing the WTO TBT Agreement, they argue this discriminates against foreign manufacturers that do not use that engine. Japan argues that cars not equipped with the best emissions-reducing technology should be targeted because they are responsible for CO_2 emissions that make it difficult for Japan to meet its obligations under the Kyoto Protocol. Japanese officials claim that the new regulation has been written flexibly, allowing EU and U.S. automakers to meet the standards however they wish, and that it does not require them to use the Mitsubishi engine, just to meet a similar level of fuel efficiency.

It remains to be seen whether the EU or the U.S. will mount a formal challenge in the WTO.

If the Kyoto Protocol—which itself doesn't contain any trade restrictions—is ruled to conflict with WTO rules, then the WTO threat to human health and environmental stability is even more urgent and direct than previously thought.

Threat 3: Europeans Weaken Ban on Cruelly Trapped Animals

The European Union has long been concerned with animal welfare issues and has enacted progressive anti-cruelty laws relating to farming, animal transport and slaughter practices. In 1991, the EU tried to extend this tradition to fur trapping but encountered threats of a WTO-challenge by the U.S. and Canada that ultimately undermined the new proposal.

The EU prohibited the use in Europe of steel jaw leg-hold traps for 13 fur bearing animals as of 1995.[30] Importation of such pelts would be banned starting in 1995 unless the exporting country forbid the use of painful steel jaw leg-hold traps or met other humane trapping standards.

North American and Russian trappers and furriers contended that these laws and rules constituted unfair trade barriers, intended to affect foreign practices (few of the species covered by the EU law were native to Europe) and discriminating against imports based on the way they were produced abroad.

After an extended period of U.S. WTO saber rattling, the EU struck a weak deal with the U.S. The proposal allowed a six-year phase-out of steel jaw leg-hold traps while the United States continues to export fur to Europe.[31] Animal welfare advocates argued that the language in the U.S.-EU agreement is sufficiently vague as to make it unenforceable.

In the future, the threatened WTO action and subsequent weak agreement could have implications for other policies concerning humane treatment of animals, such as slaughter rules, transport and testing of consumer products on laboratory animals, and fur farming techniques.

THREAT 4: U.S. THREATENS VOLUNTARY ECO-LABELING AS WTO-ILLEGAL

Eco-labels communicate product differences based on environmental or social criteria. Eco-labeling programs can be voluntary or mandatory, with certifying bodies either inside government or privately run. Familiar mandatory eco-labels with government certifications include energy ratings on appliances and the recently WTO-gutted "Dolphin Safe" label in the United States. Voluntary programs with certifications done by private organizations include the U.S. *Greenseal*, the *Nordic Swan* label and Germany's *Blue Angel*. In 1992, the European Union put in place an EU-wide voluntary eco-labeling program.[32]

In 1996, a U.S.corporate front group launched a vociferous attack against eco-labels. "The Coalition for Truth in Environmental Marketing Information" included timber, plastics, chemical, electronics and packing industry associations in addition to the Grocery Manufacturers of America and the National Food Processors Association.[33] The corporate group's main focus was to push for a U.S. position at the WTO that would effectively end voluntary eco-labeling as well as many mandatory eco-label systems by making them WTO-illegal.

In March 1996, the U.S. submitted a proposal laying out six criteria for labels to meet to be WTO-legal.[34] The proposal was revealed to be the work of corporate interests when a nearly identical six-point "Suggested Basis of U.S. Proposal Regarding Principles Applicable to Eco-labeling Programs" was accidentally released outside the U.S. government with the fax imprint of the corporate law firm that drafted it still visible. The controversy over the source of the proposal helped fuel a quick campaign by environmental and consumer groups working together as the "Save the Seals" coalition and their allies in Congress.

The proposal, drafted so broadly that it would have put Good Housekeeping Seal of Approval decisions and *Consumer Reports* ratings under WTO authority, would impose absurd and obviously unattainable standards on certifying bodies. For example, they would have to show that a program did not have the effect of "deny[ing] equivalent competitive opportunities to imports," "is not an unnecessary obstacle to international trade," and is based on a "sound science" subjective standard of evidence going beyond the TBT Agreement.[35]

The eco-labeling question was never resolved. The WTO committee considering the issue ended with intractable disagreement. However, the U.S. and Canada recently raised labeling again in the Committee on Technical Barriers to Trade with respect to proposals in Britain and other European countries to label genetically modified foods.[36] And the U.S. also has already announced it plans to challenge EU country-of-origin labeling at the WTO.[37]

Multilateral Environmental Agreements Run Afoul of WTO. Multilateral Environmental Agreements (MEAs)—covering issues ranging from climate change to air pollution, endangered species to the trade in hazardous waste—are the embodiment of global progress toward, and commitment to, the preservation of the environment. Yet many WTO rules explicitly contradict MEAs, including those in effect long before the WTO's formation.

There are several ways in which MEAs can run afoul of WTO rules. First, some of the international environmental agreements explicitly restrict trade. For instance, the Convention on International Trade in Endangered Species (CITES) bans trade in endangered species; the Basel Convention on the Transboundary Movement of Hazardous Waste bans the export of toxic waste from rich countries—which produce 98% of the world's hazardous waste—to developing nations; and the Montreal Protocol bans trade in ozone-depleting chemicals and also in products made with those chemicals. Second, these treaties and others sometimes employ the use of trade sanctions to enforce their objectives. Still other multilateral environmental agreements do not involve trade sanctions but may require countries to adopt policies that affect the potential products (asbestos, for example) of one country more than those of another. Thus, MEAs of all stripes have a significant chance of coming into conflict with GATT/WTO rules.

In addition, conflicts now have arisen between WTO rules and MEAs that don't even relate to trade. As discussed earlier, the U.S. and the EU have used WTO obligations to attack the Japanese government for strengthening its fuel efficiency laws as required under Kyoto Protocol on climate change.

Finally, unlike the WTO, which is self-executing (i.e., has built-in enforcement mechanisms), the MEAs provide commitments that each country agrees to enforce. For instance, CITES lists species for which its signatory countries have agreed that protection is needed. But, the enforcement of CITES comes not through a central CITES tribunal but rather under the domestic laws of each signatory. Thus, many U.S. CITES obligations are enforced through the Endangered Species Act (ESA). ESA provisions ban import of CITES-listed species and products made from them and endorse embargoes against countries that violate the rules. Other countries have similar domestic laws implementing their CITES obligations. Yet, under WTO rules, such domestic laws can—and have—been challenged as illegal trade barriers.

WTO dispute panels are not required to interpret the existence of MEAs as evidence in favor of environmental laws that are challenged as WTO violations. Indeed, the rules of international law stipulate that the "latest in time" of international obligations trumps previous obligations unless an exception is taken.[38] While a very limited "savings" clause—giving some precedence to three MEAs over conflicting rules—was forced into NAFTA,[39] it is conspicuously absent in the WTO or its underlying agreements. To date there have been several rulings both under GATT and the WTO that have been detrimental to domestic efforts to implement obligations undertaken under MEAs.

III. THE WTO, FOOD SAFETY STANDARDS, AND PUBLIC HEALTH

U.S. regulatory agencies have intervened in the market to save the lives of millions of Americans who otherwise would have been exposed to dangerous food, products and work environments.[1] But in their blind pursuit of increased trade volumes, new WTO rules are undermining key food safety, public health, and plant and animal health policies in the U.S. and elsewhere.

In addition to successful WTO challenges to the EU's ban on artificial beef hormone residues in meat and several other countries' quarantine laws, threats of WTO action have led South Korea to weaken two food safety rules. Outstanding WTO threats include U.S. charges against a Danish ban on lead in many products and on a Europe-wide policy on toxins in children's teething rings.

Meanwhile, WTO requirements to "harmonize" different national standards toward uniform international standards have led the U.S. to declare company-inspected beef from Australia equivalent in safety to U.S. government inspected meat. These imports can enter the U.S. labeled as if they met the U.S. law.

Finally, the WTO empowers assorted industry-influenced international organizations to set standards presumed to comply with WTO rules.

The WTO SPS Agreement: Trade Trumps Health. The WTO's Sanitary and Phytosanitary (SPS) Agreement provides parameters within which WTO Members must constrain their domestic policies concerning food safety (including contaminants, additives and food inspection), and animal and plant health (regulations with respect to pests, quarantines, and veterinary drugs).

The primary goal of the SPS Agreement is to facilitate trade by eliminating differences in food regulations that serve to fragment the global market.[2] It sets strict rules governing both permissible policy goals and the means by which nations can pursue food safety and plant and animal health goals. WTO Members can challenge each other's policies as exceeding these limits in the WTO's binding dispute resolution system.

To facilitate international uniformity in food regulations, the SPS Agreement contains a series of criteria and tests that food, animal and plant health policies must pass to be WTO-legal. First, SPS measures cannot be employed to achieve goals other than human, plant or animal life or health. A country could not, for example, ban a pesticide because it causes wild bird eggs to have thin shells and justify the ban as a legitimate SPS measure. (This was the basis for the U.S. ban on DDT.)

Second, under the SPS Agreement, the level of protection a country chooses for its citizens is a matter for WTO review—even when the standard is applied equally to domestic and foreign goods.[3] The SPS Agreement directs countries to use a technique called "risk assessment"[4] in setting their domestic food standards. Yet, some U.S. standards, for example, are based not on assessing a *tolerable* amount of risk, but in forbidding public exposure to a risk altogether. Such "zero tolerance" standards, while safer for consumers, are inherently problematic under WTO rules because they are not developed using the version of risk assessment approved by the WTO.

LORI WALLACH & MICHELLE SFORZA

Third, the SPS Agreement sharply restricts the right of countries to adopt or maintain standards that exceed those promulgated by international bodies.[5] The WTO empowers specific, named international standard-setting agencies to create standards for food safety and plant and animal health (as well as product safety and technical standards).

Unfortunately, these standard-setting bodies—the Codex Alimentarius in the case of food safety and the International Organization on Standardization (ISO) in the case of technical, product and environmental standards—are dominated by industry and operate in a closed manner, insulated from public oversight or accountability. (Indeed, the ISO is a purely private-sector organization.) Not surprisingly, they tend to set weaker standards than those set by governments with strong, open participatory policymaking.

To maintain regulations more stringent than the international standards, countries must overcome high hurdles. They must prove that the level of protection they set meets WTO requirements and that there is no other way to achieve their WTO-legal goal without affecting trade. The WTO SPS rules have the cumulative effect of eliminating differences in national laws and also limiting the strength of food safety protections.

WTO Record On Food Safety and Quarantine Laws. After five years, a trend in the food arena has emerged. WTO panels have ruled against all food safety and plant or animal quarantine laws regulations under review on the grounds that they restrict trade more than necessary. These include the EU's consumer protection ban on artificial hormone-treated beef, Japan's testing requirements designed to keep fruit pests out of the country and Australia's quarantine on raw salmon imports, which was designed to protect the health of indigenous fish population. The Australian salmon case was notable for an Appellate Body holding that costly and time-consuming risk assessments which specify the precise, quantified risk to animals or plants must be conducted each time *prior* to a WTO Member's introduction or enforcement of a regulation relating to plant and animal pests and diseases.[6]

CASE 1: THE WTO INSISTS EUROPE ACCEPT ARTIFICIAL HORMONE-TREATED BEEF

In a major defeat for health and safety policies based on the premise that potentially dangerous substances should be proven safe before they are marketed, a WTO panel ruled in 1997 against an EU ban on artificial hormone-treated beef.

Since 1988, the EU has banned the sale of beef from cattle treated with artificial hormones and has applied the ban in a nondiscriminatory fashion to both domestic and imported beef products.[7] Exposure to the artificial hormones themselves have been linked to cancer and premature pubescence in girls,[8] although the risk to humans of artificial hormone residues in the meat they consume has yet to be conclusively measured. Rather than trying to assess a tolerable amount of an indeterminable risk or waiting for negative human health affects to accrue over time, the EU chose to eliminate public exposure to the risk altogether.

The U.S. beef and biotechnology industries have long opposed this EU policy.[9] In January 1996, the U.S. challenged the ban at the WTO.[10] In 1998, a WTO panel ruled that the beef hormone ban was an illegal measure under SPS rules in part because it was not based on a WTO-approved risk assessment.[11] The WTO Appellate Body affirmed the original panel's decision, and the EU was ordered to begin imports of U.S. artificial hormone-treated beef by May 13, 1999.[12]

After the EU refused to comply with the WTO panel ruling by the May 1999 deadline, the WTO on July 12, 1999, approved a U.S. request to impose retaliatory sanctions against European-made products.[13]

In its beef hormone ruling, the WTO effectively declared that food safety regulations enacted in advance of scientific certainty were not allowed. The WTO in effect attempted to eliminate from the standard-setting process such factors as the cultural values, attitudes and priorities of individual societies, as well as the desire to shield people from unnecessary exposure to potentially dangerous substances. The WTO ruling in this case poses a direct challenge to one of the pillars of contemporary public health policy, the Precautionary Principle. Under this principle, potentially dangerous substances must be proven safe before they are put on the market

The WTO stood the Precautionary Principle on its head, shifting—from the manufacturer to the government—the burden of proof that a product is safe. Under the WTO rule, government must scientifically prove a product is dangerous before it can regulate that product. By rejecting a popular consumer safeguard solidly grounded in the Precautionary Principle, the WTO made a powerful statement about its priorities.

THREAT 1: U.S. THREAT OVER EU TOXIC TEETHING RING BAN BACKFIRES

In an attempt to limit the exposure of infants to toxic substances in their toys, the EU moved to regulate the prevalence of certain chemicals in children's toys, especially teethers and toys that are put into the mouth, by restricting potentially toxic phthalates, the additive that makes hard plastics pliable instead of brittle, and labeling the content of the toys.[14] American toy producers suggested that the proposal may be an illegal barrier to trade.[15]

With information on health risks accumulating, several European countries recommended that industry voluntarily stop using plastic softeners in toys marketed to children under three years by 1997;[16] others considered legislative bans.

Concerned, the "leading toy manufacturers contacted the Commerce Department ... to rectify a problem,"[17] according to a State Department memo. The State Department memo, sent to European station chiefs, suggested that the Europeans were being too stringent and noted that Americans already limit phthalates in toys. The memo noted that the Toy Manufacturers of America voluntarily limits phthlates to 3% in pacifiers and teethers. The memo went on to criticize the marketing ban for exceeding the U.S. standard.

The State Department alert urged the consulates and embassies to press for a withdrawal of the marketing bans "in time for the Christmas purchasing season."[18] The *Los Angeles Times* reported that the Clinton administration was "acting at the behest of Mattel Inc. and other[s]."[19]

But a pressure campaign by Greenpeace and others built such strong support for action that the Europeans refused to be intimidated. In July 1999, the EU decided to let Members regulate phthalates on a nation-by-nation basis.[20] And the toy industry has announced it would begin phasing out pthalates from those products designed to be put in the mouths of children and infants.[21]

IV. THE WTO'S IMPACT ON EMERGING HEALTH AND ENVIRONMENTAL ISSUES

Genetically Modified Organisms. GMOs are new varieties of living organisms created when scientists splice the genes of two different species in an attempt to produce a new species with certain desirable characteristics. Multinational corporations, such as Monsanto, Novartis, Dupont and Avantis, have applied this process primarily to agricultural crops, including cotton, soya and corn, to improve resistance to disease, pesticides and herbicides, enhance nutritional value and increase yield.[1]

In the U.S., products containing GMOs are completely unregulated. Consumers have no idea which products contain GMOs, and no way of knowing what threats GMOs pose to human health.

However, a growing body of evidence suggests serious

health risks from GMOs, as well as environmental harms ranging from threats to the monarch butterfly to incursions on biodiversity as genetically engineered crops pass traits to the remaining natural crops.

GMO technology raises serious public interest concerns in many areas where the WTO has proven most hostile: food security and safety, ecological sustainability and environmental protection. Thus, a future conflict over GMO regulations could become emblematic of the WTO's emerging pattern of tying the hands of policymakers who wish to stand firmly on the side of caution, public safety and the environment, and regulate the trade of such products until more is learned about their impacts.

Three WTO agreements may make it difficult for countries to maintain or strengthen their domestic safeguards regarding GMOs: the Agreement on Sanitary and Phytosanity Measures (SPS), the Agreement on Technical Barriers to Trade (TBT) and the Agreement on Trade Related Aspects of Intellectual Property Rights (TRIPs). The first two agreements put heavy burdens on governments wishing to restrict the entry of products containing GMOs into their countries. The SPS Agreement requires that the GMO-regulating nation provide scientific data proving a threat to justify a regulation,[2] even though the lack of scientific certainty concerning GMO impacts is precisely why governments have begun to regulate them. The TBT Agreement requires governments to minimize trade impacts when setting standards regulating products, including GMO products, under the least trade restrictive rule.[3] In addition, the U.S. claims that the mere labeling of a product to identify it as containing GMOs may fall under TBT rules, possibly undermining even this relatively modest form of product regulation. The TRIPs Agreement allows GMO agricultural products to be patented, creating new commercial rights for such products that may conflict with government policy goals regarding biodiversity and food security.

U.S. Trade Demands Jam Biosafety Protocol Talks.
Reflecting the growing international concern with the possible risks of GMOs, representatives of more than 140 nations met in Cartagena, Colombia, in February 1999 for ten days to complete a Biosafety Protocol covering GMOs.[4] The conference was to be the culmination of almost seven years of international effort among countries to formulate a policy to safeguard the public against a technology whose long-term effects are essentially unstudied.

The U.S.-led[5] "Miami Group," composed of major exporters of GMOs, including Canada, Argentina, Chile and Australia, however, wanted to protect industry interests by writing into the Biosafety Protocol the WTO SPS Agreement provisions requiring nations seeking to prohibit GMOs to justify their decisions on "sound science."[6] Limits on trade based on unproven biosafety concerns, the U.S. argued, should be considered barriers to trade, and the Protocol should explicitly mention that WTO rules prevail over the Protocol.[7]

In the end, the Miami Group blocked adoption of the Biosafety Protocol by refusing to include commodities (e.g. soya and corn) in the negotiations,[8] even though commodities represent the vast bulk of GMOs the treaty was designed to cover.

GMO Regulations Proliferate While U.S. Explicitly Threatens WTO Action. Despite the U.S. sabotage of the Biosafety Protocol signing, in increasing numbers nations are taking steps to regulate GMOs. As early as 1992, the EU had approved a voluntary labeling scheme. Then, in May 1997, the EU adopted the "Novel Foods Regulation" requiring labeling of all new processed foods and food ingredients, including those made with GMOs. In September 1998, an EU policy requiring the labeling of genetically modified corn and soybeans went into effect. The June 1999 amendments to the EU Directive on Deliberate Release of Genetically Modified Organisms included a broad mandatory labeling scheme.[9]

LORI WALLACH & MICHELLE SFORZA

The U.S. considers such regulations to be unnecessary and also illegal barriers to trade.[10]

Rather than requiring extensive testing of GMOs at the expense of the U.S. agribusiness industry, the U.S. government instead has tried to downwardly "harmonize" GMO regulations adopted by the rest of the world to the U.S. "non-standard." For example, after the EU rejected Monsanto's application to market two genetically engineered cotton seeds, Frank Loy, U.S. undersecretary of state for global affairs, reserved the right to challenge the decision in the WTO because, he claimed, the EU's decision was not based on "sound science."[11]

Despite the U.S.'s admission that it has not researched the safety of GMO products,[12] the U.S. continues to insist that GMO regulations proposed and enacted around the world may be WTO-illegal because GMOs have not yet been proven dangerous. Unfortunately, nations desiring to prohibit, restrict or even label GMOs could be vulnerable to a successful U.S. WTO challenge because the WTO SPS and TBT Agreements contain the same backwards logic.

U.S. Industry Pushing for New Biotechnology Rights and Protections at Seattle. Despite the growing global consensus in favor of GMO regulation, the U.S. industry and the Clinton administration are seeking to strengthen the existing WTO constraints on government action in this area. The "built-in" agenda for the Seattle Ministerial (items agreed to at past negotiations) includes a revision of the Agreement on Agriculture. Thus, issues of food safety and GMOs are sure to surface in Seattle.

The U.S. and Canada—home to giant biotechnology companies such as Monsanto and DuPont/Pioneer—also have announced that they will push to *add* new protections for trade of biotechnology products to the Seattle agenda. The issue may come as an addition to an existing agreements or as a new stand-alone agreement on biotechnology. A concrete goal for both countries is to reduce the approval process time in other WTO Member countries on imports containing GMOs.[13]

V. WTO INTELLECTUAL PROPERTY RIGHTS, ACCESS TO MEDICINES AND PATENTS ON LIFE

Intellectual Property Rights, or IPRs, bestow ownership rights and legal protections on ideas, artistic creations (such as novels, music and films), technological innovations and marketing tools (logos and trademarks, for instance). The WTO Agreement on Trade Related Aspects of Intellectual Property (TRIPs) establishes enforceable global property rights and requires all 134 WTO Members to enact domestic legislation to enforce these new rights.

The level of IPR protection required by the TRIPs Agreement is extremely high—higher than most WTO Members had in place before implementing the Uruguay Round Agreements—and broad in its scope, covering pharmaceuticals, agricultural chemicals, plant varieties and seed germplasms, including those resulting from generations of plant breeding and traditional remedies, microorganisms and much more. The WTO TRIPS Agreement, instead of promoting "free trade" established a 20-year monopoly marketing right for patent holders. This WTO rule required the U.S. to extend its patent protections from 17 to 20 years, a move which was conservatively calculated to cost U.S. consumers $6 billion given the delay in availability of generic versions of many medicines.[1]

The WTO TRIPs Agreement: Developing Country Access to Food and Medicine. The TRIPs Agreement has created a firestorm of protest in the developing world. Many developing countries have traditionally excluded food and medicine from their IPR laws in order to ensure that these basic necessities are accessible and affordable and not subject to private monopoly control. Under the TRIPs Agreement, however, what was once in the public domain—food and medicine—must now be privatized through global patent law. From the perspective of many in the developing world, where food shortages and disease threaten the population on an ongoing basis, WTO TRIPs protections for corporate property rights outrageously undermine the ability of governments to respond generally to basic public needs and specifically to public health crises.

The WTO TRIPs Rules Endanger Food Security. The TRIPs Agreement further undermines precarious worldwide food security by exacerbating food and seed access and distribution problems. One provision requires that WTO Members protect agribusiness ownership over plant varieties, including seeds. This requirement provides dramatic new tools to consolidate the power of large seed and biotechnology manufacturers by shifting ownership and control of seed stocks away from farmers.

When corporations patent seeds, local farmers must pay annual fees to use the seed type, even if the seed was the product of breeding conducted over generations by the very ancestors of the farmers themselves. So far, patents have been awarded on varieties of soybeans, corn and canola.[2] Subsistence farmers can ill-afford to pay the cost of purchasing seed each year. On the other hand, the TRIPs Agreement contains no protections for indigenous communities that have been planting and crossbreeding strains for centuries to develop that perfectly adapted variety that a bioprospector can collect and have patented to some distant corporation.

Monopoly ownership over crop varieties as encouraged by the TRIPs Agreement has also been linked to the spread of "mono-culture agriculture." Aggressive marketing of the products protected by intellectual property rights can lead to the spread of the same variety of crop or livestock worldwide and to the displacement of hundreds of local varieties of crops and breeds of livestock.[3] Monocultures are dangerously unstable ecosystems that have lost their diversity and hence their resistance against pests, diseases and environmental stresses. The deadly Irish potato famine resulted in part from mono-cropping. The potato blight was able to move from field to field throughout the country because of reliance on one variety of potato, the lumper.

WTO TRIPs Agreement Facilitates Biopiracy of Developing Country Resources. Biopiracy is commercial appropriation of plants, seeds, herbs or traditional processes for obtaining medicinal or pesticidal benefits from local flora and fauna that rural and indigenous communities have been cultivating or using for hundreds or even thousands of years. Corporations appropriate, patent, and profit from indigenous knowledge without any benefits returning to the communities from which the plants originated. To earn the right to patent a plant, companies merely must claim that they have altered the plant, even if that alteration does not change the plant in any meaningful way.[4] Since patent examiners often do not have access to facilities to test the alleged "new trait," the patent is often granted and validity of the claim is left to civil litigation, which is too costly for indigenous communities to undertake.[5]

Once the TRIPs Agreement is fully phased in, developing country WTO Members will have the obligation to enforce seed companies' patent rights by either uprooting "illegal" crops or collecting the fees from subsistence farmers. Failure to do so would leave the country in violation of its TRIPs obligations and susceptible to trade sanctions.[6]

The first famous example of biopiracy involves patents on certain products derived from the neem tree, which is native to India. The indigenous population in India has always revered the tree for its medicinal value and use as a biopesticide.[7] Nicknamed "the village pharmacy," for centuries people in India have used products derived from the tree for cleaning teeth and treating conditions ranging from acne to ulcers.[8]

Since 1971, when a U.S. importer observed the tree's pharmaceutical properties, multinational corporations from the U.S. and Japan have sought and been granted numerous patents on various products extracted from the neem tree.[9] The U.S.-incorporated W.R. Grace Company has already started manufacturing and commercializing its neem products by establishing a base in India.[10] Grace's justification for its patent is that its modernized extraction processes constitute a genuine innovation.[11] It matters little that the so-called innovation was based on traditional knowledge and that neem-based biopesticides and medicines have been produced by indigenous populations, many using complex processes for centuries.

With its patent claim under challenge, the W.R. Grace Company is expected to defend its right to patent the traditional pesticide—and to emphasize India's obligation to protect its patent—under the TRIPs Agreement.[12]

Thailand introduced legislation in 1997 to prevent future neem-like biopiracy incidents within its borders. It proposed to establish a process for Thai traditional healers to register their traditional medicines so that, in the event that a biotechnology or pharmaceutical company sought a patent on the substance or process, the company would have to negotiate with the traditional healer.[13] In response to the proposal, the U.S. State Department sent a letter in April 1997 to the Royal Thai Government (RTG) warning that "Washington believes that such a registration system could constitute a possible violation of the TRIPs Agreement and hamper medical research into these compounds."[14]

To date, the Thai government has not heeded the U.S. threat, and the legislation is currently making its way through Parliament.

The TRIPs Agreement, Pharmaceuticals and Health.

THREAT 1: U.S., GERBER TRADE THREATS PRESSURE GUATEMALA TO WEAKEN INFANT FORMULA LAW

In an attempt to reduce its infant mortality rate, Guatemala passed a law and issued regulations in 1983 designed to encourage new mothers to breast feed their infants and to fully understand the health threats to their babies of using infant formula as a substitute for breast milk. The law, which implemented the terms of the WHO/ UNICEF Code on Marketing of Breast-Milk Substitutes, included prohibitions on the use of words like "humanized breast milk" or "equivalent to breast milk."[15] To be accessible to illiterate people, the WHO/ UNICEF Code and Guatemala's regulations also included prohibitions against visual depictions of infants that "idealize the use of bottle feeding."[16]

One infant formula producer, Gerber Food® (Gerber), bridled at the Guatemalan law and its regulations because the company's trademarked logo includes the picture of a pudgy infant, the "Gerber Baby." Shortly before the Uruguay Round's effective date, a Gerber vice president wrote to Guatemala's president, implicitly threatening some form of trade sanctions.[17] The dispute pit a nation trying to protect its most vulnerable citizens, its newborns, against a transnational food producer (motto: "Babies are our business"[18]) insistent not only on selling infant formula but in marketing its products in a manner that Guatemalan law deemed misleading.

According to UNICEF, 1.5 million infants die each year because their mothers are induced to replace breast feeding with artificial breast milk substitutes.[19] UNICEF reports that the major cause of death is fatal infant diarrhea caused by mothers in poor countries mixing the infant formula with unclean water.[20] UNICEF attributes the fact that only 44% of infants in the developing world (even less in the industrialized countries) are breast-fed to the relentless promotion of breast milk substitutes.[21]

With the prominent exception of U.S.-incorporated Gerber, all of Guatemala's domestic and foreign suppliers of infant formula and other breast milk substitutes made the necessary changes to their packaging to comply with the Guatemalan law.[22] Guatemalan infant mortality rates

LORI WALLACH & MICHELLE SFORZA

dropped significantly after the law passed, and UNICEF held up Guatemala as a model of the Code's success in its literature.[23]

But Gerber refused to comply with the Guatemalan law, warning that Guatemala would likely face a WTO challenge if it did not repeal the rule. In fact, a special public health exception in the TRIPS agreement probably would have safeguarded Guatemala's actions.

But Guatemala had no in-house expertise on the question of the WTO legality of its implementation of the WHO/UNICEF Code.[24] By 1995, Gerber's threats of WTO action, taken seriously by the Guatemalan government at home and at its Washington embassy, succeeded. Guatemala changed the law so that imported baby food products would be exempt from Guatemala's stringent infant food labeling policy.[25]

THREAT 2: PHARMACEUTICAL INDUSTRY THREATENS WTO CHALLENGE OVER SOUTH AFRICAN MEDICINE LAW

The TRIPs Agreement requires WTO Member countries to have in place 20-year IPR protections for pharmaceutical prices by 2005. Patents give pharmaceutical companies the exclusive right to market a particular medication. However, the TRIPS agreement does contain important caveats—such as permitting compulsory licensing and parallel imports—designed to allow governments to modify some patent holders' rights in the name of promoting public welfare. Under compulsory licensing, governments require patent holders to license drugs or other goods to competing manufacturers in exchange for royalty payments to the drug's developer. Parallel importing is the practice of importing goods through wholesalers or other third-party intermediaries from countries where goods are cheaper, rather than buying directly from the manufacturer.

Governments adopt parallel importing policies because pharmaceutical prices can vary wildly among countries. For instance, the antibiotic Amoxicillin costs 50 cents a tablet in South Africa compared to 4 cents each in neighboring Zimbabwe.

Despite these important public health provisions included in the TRIPS, the international pharmaceutical industry, with assistance from the Clinton administration, has tried to use TRIPS to reverse the effort by former South African President Nelson Mandela to make health care and medicines more accessible for South Africans. The South African Medicines Law, enacted in 1997 but not yet fully implemented, would encourage the use of generic drugs and prohibit pharmaceutical companies from paying doctors bounties for prescribing their products (already illegal in the U.S. under anti-kickback laws). Most notably, it would institute parallel importing and permit compulsory licensing as a means to control pharmaceuticals costs.[26]

The South African and U.S. pharmaceutical industries present a united front in opposition to the South African law with the head of the South African Pharmaceutical Manufacturers' Association (PMA) having threatened the South African government with a WTO challenge.[27]

The U.S. government joined them, undertaking a "full-court press" against the South African law, in the words of a State Department memo.[28] High level officials, including Vice President Al Gore, repeatedly raised the issue with South African policymakers.[29] The U.S. imposed or threatened to impose trade and other sanctions against South Africa.

South Africa, however, refused to back down. A pressure campaign, led by AIDS activists who realized how South Africa's efforts to lower drug prices could help make AIDS medicines available to South Africa's skyrocketing population of people with HIV/AIDS, forced the U.S. to back off of its threats against South Africa. It remains to be seen whether the U.S. will respect other countries' right to use compulsory licensing and parallel imports.

VI. THE WTO AND DEVELOPING COUNTRIES

At the conclusion of the Uruguay Round negotiations in 1994, developing countries were promised they would experience major gains as industrialized countries lowered and eventually eliminated tariffs on such items as textiles and apparel and cut agricultural subsidies that enabled them to dominate world commodity markets.

Yet contrary to this rosy scenario, after nearly five years of the WTO, the share of the pie for most of the world's population living in developing countries got smaller, and that smaller portion was divided even less equally among individuals.

First, the Least Developed Countries' (LDCs) share of world exports and imports has fallen sharply since the Uruguay Round, according to the United Nations Commission on Trade and Development (UNCTAD).[1] According to UNCTAD, as a result of the implementation of the Uruguay Round accords, the world's poorest nations—the 47 least developed countries—will lose an estimated $163 billion to $265 billion in export earnings while paying $145 million to $292 million more for food imports.[2]

UNCTAD concludes that LDCs continue to be marginalized in world trade not because of any resistance to openness but because of their inability to expand productive capacity.[3] Uruguay Round Agreements that transformed core components of economic development policy into trade law violations will compound this problem. For instance, the prohibition on some tariffs for imported manufactured goods being sent to poor countries forces nascent industry to compete with vastly more productive foreign manufacturers, thus stunting domestic industrial development in the LDCs.

Second, as developing countries have deregulated and opened up their economies under the orders of the International Monetary Fund (IMF) and in line with the policy prescriptions of WTO proponents, most have seen sharp declines in their rates of growth.[4]

Third, while the world's largest corporations have generated record earnings,[5] income inequality has increased between and within countries since the WTO's implementation. As mentioned earlier, the income gap between the fifth of the world's people living in the richest countries and the fifth in the poorest was 74-to-1 in 1997, up from 60-to-1 in 1990 and 30-to-1 in 1960.[6]

Uruguay Round Agreements Include Provisions Especially Threatening to Developing Countries. The WTO didn't create world poverty, of course, and it can only be given a small share of the blame for the worsening trends that date back a decade and a half prior to the WTO's establishment. But several specific concepts and provisions in the Uruguay Round package have made things worse economically for developing countries.

Systematic Tariff Escalation Promotes "Rip and Ship" Natural Resources Use. Uruguay Round tariff schedules provide for the escalation of tariff rates as value is added to a product. The tariff rate increases with processing and manufacturing, thus, the lowest rate is for a raw commodity.

This Uruguay Round feature is one reason developing country WTO critics say the Uruguay Round promotes economic "recolonization" of developing countries that only recently gained political independence. Tariff escalation creates an incentive for "rip and ship" natural resource exploitation in poor countries. Exports facing tariff escalation and the WTO's ban on the use of high tariffs to protect infant industries in developing countries from competing imports produced by more established firms in rich countries discourages LDCs from further industrialization. Thus, furniture produced in a developing country from that country's tropical wood and exported for sale in a developed country faces a relatively high tariff. Raw tropical timber logs shipped into the rich country face relatively lower tariffs, and when the furniture is produced in the rich country from that wood, it faces no additional tariff mark-up.

Under the Uruguay Round tariff schedule, by 2000, tariffs are to be eliminated in many commodities that currently represent a substantial export income for the world's poorest countries.[7] These include coffee, tea, cocoa beans, metal ores, cotton, gold, diamonds and fresh vegetables.

Falling Commodity Prices Undermine Food Security. Primary commodity prices already have fallen by 25% since 1995, the year the WTO went into effect, and now are at historic lows.[8] Compounding the problem of lower export earnings caused by plunging commodity prices is the fact that least developed countries have become net importers of food and therefore must have a steady stream of foreign exchange simply to finance the *imports* needed to feed the population.

The Uruguay Round Agriculture Agreement prohibited numerous internal support programs and import controls that developing countries typically use to protect small producers and encourage self-sufficiency in food production[9] while permitting continuing export subsidies.[10] With small local producers no longer shielded from the subsidized agricultural commodities of the U.S. and particularly the EU, the Uruguay Round creates increased dependency on imported staples like wheat and corn.

CASE 1: U.S. ATTACKS CARIBBEAN BANANAS FOR CHIQUITA
The Lomé Convention between the EU and its former colonies in Africa, the Caribbean and the Pacific (ACP countries) establishes preferential tariffs and sets aside some portion of the EU market for the ACP countries for a set list of products.[11] This regime is considered indispensable for the economic and political stability of the ACP countries.[12] The EU negotiated a waiver for the Lomé Convention for Uruguay Round Most Favored Nation (MFN) tariff require-

ments. In 1996, the U.S. government, on behalf of the U.S. corporation Chiquita Brands International (Chiquita), challenged the EU policy under the Lomé Convention of setting aside a portion of its banana market for Caribbean Island producers.

While most of the world's bananas are grown for Chiquita, Del Monte and Dole on large Latin and Central American plantations that rely on cheap farm labor,[13] Eastern Caribbean banana producers, in contrast, tend to be small-scale farmers who own and work small plots of mountainous land and whose production costs are therefore higher.

Bananas are central to the economic and political stability of several small Caribbean island nations, where mountainous terrain and limited arable land make cultivation of other legal cash crops impossible. The ACP countries most dependent upon the Lomé Convention banana regimes include the Windward Islands nations of St. Lucia, Dominica, St. Vincent and the Grenadines, where banana production accounts for between 63% and 91% of export earnings.[14]

The U.S. filed its challenge against the EU even though it does not produce a single banana for trade. Some speculate the decision to mount the WTO challenge—which ultimately proved successful—was due to the large campaign contributions that Chiquita and its chairman Carl Lindner have made to both major parties.[15]

When the EU delayed the WTO-ordered elimination of its Caribbean banana program, the U.S. in March 1999 imposed trade sanctions against the EU worth $190 million annually.[16]

If the EU decides to lift is protections for the Caribbean banana producers, the Caribbean banana economy will collapse completely. There is widespread acknowledgment that one consequence of such a collapse would be a surge in illegal drug cultivation and trafficking.[17]

LORI WALLACH & MICHELLE SFORZA

VII. HUMAN AND LABOR RIGHTS UNDER THE WTO

The Uruguay Round Agreements, when taken as a whole, create a system of global commerce shaped to serve large multinational corporations with the resources to move production around the world and to provide goods and/or services to numerous markets simultaneously. The rights of workers are completely ignored, except to the extent that government policies promoting workers' rights are considered barriers to trade and therefore are subject to attack under WTO rules.

Similarly, differential treatment of countries based on their human rights records is explicitly forbidden. Thus, the sort of sanctions requested by South African leaders in the struggle against apartheid would have seriously conflicted with the current WTO rules. Already one U.S. state's selective purchasing law against the Burmese military dictatorship has been challenged under WTO rules.

No Labor Rights at the WTO. The WTO Trade Related Investment Measures (TRIMs) rules encourage the spread of export processing zones (EPZs), where global manufacturing firms import most of their components from overseas subsidiaries and pay production workers starvation wages to assemble the products for export for sale in rich markets.

The low-wage EPZ scenario is promoted by a combination of WTO rules that forbid the sorts of countermeasures governments would need to take to ensure both labor rights protections and more diversified production. For example, the WTO TRIMs Agreement forbids developing country governments from requiring that a certain portion of a product's content be procured domestically. Doing so would create more jobs besides those needed to simply assemble products to export to rich countries. Nor do WTO rules permit importing countries to close their borders to goods made in factories or countries where worker rights are violated.

The prospects for rectifying the WTO's bias against workers *vis-a-vis* multinational corporations through any reform of the WTO are slim. In 1994, during the Uruguay Round negotiations, the U.S. and France had suggested that a "social clause" should be included in the WTO.[1] These half-hearted efforts failed, as have all subsequent efforts.

In any case, many nongovernmental organizations most involved with globalization issues actually view the notion of a WTO "social clause" as useless and politically damaging at best, and as a dangerous distraction from the WTO's real problems, at worst. The basic argument of these groups is that without actually changing or eliminating the numerous core WTO principles and rules that undermine the public interest, adding pro-labor or other language is like putting a bandage over gangrene. The same damage will continue unabated, but it might draw less attention in the short term.

WTO Challenges Threaten Basic Labor and Human Rights. The WTO now also is being used as an aggressive tool to attack strong occupational safeguards as described below in the case of Canada's WTO challenge of the new French asbestos ban. In addition, WTO rules have been used—both in a challenge and as threats—to discourage governments from using their purchasing power to combat brutal dictatorships and human rights violators.

CASE 1: CANADA ATTACKS FRENCH ASBESTOS BAN AT WTO

In 1996, France joined Germany, Austria, Denmark, the Netherlands, Finland, Italy, Sweden and Belgium to ban all forms of asbestos,[2] a product that causes deadly asbestosis and cancer.

The French law bans asbestos and any product containing it, unless the use of asbestos substitutes would pose a graver public health risk. The ban applies to domestic production as well as to the import of asbestos.

Canada, the second-largest exporter of asbestos in the

world,[3] challenged the French ban in the WTO in 1998 as a violation of the WTO Technical Barriers to Trade (TBT) Agreement and of GATT rules banning quantitative restrictions on imports and forbidding discriminatory trade measures.[4]

Canada claims that less trade-restrictive measures are available to protect workers from the ill effects of asbestos, making a *ban* impermissible under the TBT Agreement. It asserts that chrysotile asbestos is less harmful than other types of asbestos and that it can be used without incurring any detectable risk. Canada therefore argues that an alternative form of regulation exists that will satisfy the French objective to safeguard public health—that of "controlled use."

In its complaint to the WTO, Canada also points to international standards that support the "controlled use" form of regulating asbestos, though public health advocates point out that the asbestos industry has decisively influenced these standards. WTO rules require use of international standards with very limited exceptions. Canada cites as the presumptive WTO legal standard for regulating asbestos the International Organization on Standardization (ISO) guidelines for working with chrysotile asbestos,[5] even though the ISO is an industry-funded, industry-membership group.

Many people view the prospects of a WTO ruling against an asbestos ban as a massive blow against the universally recognized right to a safe workplace contained in International Labor Organization conventions and other treaties. According to the World Health Organization, there are already 160 million cases a year of occupational disease worldwide.[6] This epidemic points to a broad problem of lax enforcement—or no enforcement at all—of occupational health and safety laws. If the WTO were to rule against a public health ban of a proven carcinogen present in numerous countries, the future of many other hard-earned laws aimed at ensuring a safe workplace will also be put at risk.

CASE 2: WTO CHALLENGE OF LAW TARGETING BURMESE MILITARY DICTATORSHIP'S HUMAN RIGHTS ABUSES

The serious human rights violations and the deliberate suppression of democracy perpetrated by the military junta ruling Burma (which the junta has renamed Myanmar) since it came to power in 1988 are well known throughout the world. Burma's pro-democracy movement, led by Nobel Peace Prize holder Aung San Suu Kyi, has called for South Africa-style foreign divestment from Burma to financially starve the military dictatorship.[7] Some two dozen U.S. municipal and county governments, and the state government of Massachusetts[8] have acted on this request and terminated purchasing contracts with companies doing business in Burma. The selective purchasing laws are designed to ensure that public money is not used to indirectly support a regime whose conduct taxpayers find repugnant. A goal of such policies is to create incentives to encourage transnational corporations to divest from Burma.

The corporate attack launched in response to the Massachusetts' selective purchasing law was two-pronged. Japan and the EU pressed a case in the WTO, arguing the Massachusetts law violated the WTO Agreement on Government Procurement and its requirement that governments base purchasing decisions solely on quality and price determinations. Meanwhile, a front group for multinational corporations called USA*Engage[9] challenged the measure in Massachusetts state court as a violation of the U.S. Constitution. Federal district and appellate courts have sided with the business group's claim that the Massachusetts law interfered with the executive branch's exclusive authority to conduct foreign policy, so for now the EU and Japanese WTO challenge is in abeyance.

Even so, the EU-Japan WTO challenge has already claimed a casualty. The Clinton administration, concerned about another WTO suit and the bad press it would generate, launched a successful campaign against a similar Maryland human rights proposal aimed at Nigeria. A State

Department official testified against the proposal, citing WTO concerns, and helped turn the tide against the selective purchasing legislation, which unexpectedly was defeated by one vote.

VIII. DEMANDS AND CONCLUSIONS

The Uruguay Round and WTO have failed the most conservative of tests: to do no further damage. Instead, in the key areas of public health, enforcement protection, economic development and food security, conditions have seriously deteriorated as a direct result of WTO rules.

What is truly alarming is that for many developing countries, fallout from the harshest of the WTO rules is still to come, because the rules have multi-year phase-ins and are not yet fully implemented. In an acknowledgment of the damage already done by WTO rules, many developing countries' governments and non-governmental organizations oppose the European call for a new and comprehensive round of WTO talks and instead have called for a "turnaround" to undo the damage being wrought by the current WTO regime.

Indeed, there are indications of serious problems in virtually every key area where the U.S. and other governments promised their citizens WTO benefits. The world has been buffeted by unprecedented global financial instability. Income inequality is increasing rapidly between and within countries. Despite efficiency and productivity gains, wages in numerous countries have failed to rise, while commodity prices are at an all-time low, causing a decrease in the standard of living for a majority of people in the world.

The WTO's built-in bias against public participation has made the institution a perfect venue for industry and governments to pursue agendas that would fail in open democratic forums. One WTO bureaucrat admitted this to the *Financial Times*, stating the WTO "is the place where governments collude in private against their domestic pressure groups."[1]

Despite this compelling evidence, the EU in 1999 was leading a charge to launch an ambitious new round of negotiations to extend the WTO's constraints on government action to new issues. One EU proposal was to revive the failed Multilateral Agreement on Investment (MAI) by putting it into the WTO.[2] Japan has supported the EU initiative on launching a new round, as has the Canadian government.

The Clinton administration has never been eager for a long, drawn-out round of negotiations. First, it has been stripped both of Fast Track trade authority and congressional and public support for its radical globalization agenda. Second, it did not want Vice President Al Gore's record of sacrificing environmental goals on the altar of globalization to be highlighted before the 2000 presidential election. Thus the U.S. has promoted a so-called "modest" agenda, which calls for extreme agriculture and forestry liberalization, further expansion of WTO coverage and deregulation in the services sector (including health and education), and new guarantees that biotechnology products must be accepted worldwide.

The year-long investigation we conducted to write our book *Whose Trade Organization?* does not purport to be a comprehensive compilation of the WTO's problems, yet it has clearly shown that the five-year record of the WTO does not support the launch of a new comprehensive round of WTO expansion talks. Rather, our review documents the urgent need for a 180-degree turnaround of badly flawed, major elements of the current GATT/WTO regime.

While groups such as Public Citizen support enforceable international commercial rules to govern the flow of goods and services, we advocate having no tolerance for such rules being used to further undermine democratic, accountable governance or public interest safeguards. There is a growing consensus among nongovernmental organizations

LORI WALLACH & MICHELLE SFORZA

(NGOs) worldwide that the WTO must be pruned back to ensure:

➤ access to essential goods, such as food and medicines;

➤ access to essential services, such as safe water, sanitation and other utilities, education, transportation and health care;

➤ respect for basic labor and other human rights;

➤ product, food and workplace safety;

➤ a healthy environment and conservation of natural resources;

➤ the availability of information, such as the accurate labeling of the contents and characteristics of goods;

➤ choice among competitively priced goods and services;

➤ representation of citizen interests in decision-making; and

➤ an avenue of redress, including the ability to hold accountable corporations and governments that undermine core citizens' rights.

A reasonable interim step, and one that could be agreed upon at the November 1999 Seattle WTO Ministerial, is the nearly unanimous call by nongovernmental organizations worldwide for the thorough review of the WTO's performance to date rather than the launch of *further* trade or investment liberalization negotiations.

WTO rules should not be extended to cover new issues such as investment (MAI), and corporate control in existing agreements (such as the U.S. proposal to add all life forms to the definition of "property" under the existing WTO TRIPs Agreement) should not be widened. Rather, at the Seattle Ministerial, governments must agree to a comprehensive review of the outcomes and impacts of the Uruguay Round to date with an eye toward identifying which aspects should be scaled back, replaced or eliminated.

We urgently advocate that The Seattle Ministerial Declaration include the following:

SEATTLE MINISTERIAL DECLARATION: 7 DEMANDS

1. Enact A Moratorium on Certain Trade Challenges. Given the troubling pattern of WTO rulings against domestic food safety, environmental and health measures, the WTO Member governments must agree in the Seattle Ministerial Declaration to impose a moratorium on WTO challenges and threats to facially nondiscriminatory environmental, health and safety measures. Challenges to domestic laws based on the level of protection a country chooses (such as France's asbestos ban) or based on countries acting under the Precautionary Principle (such as the EU ban on beef containing artificial hormone residues) must stop. A moratorium also would forestall challenges to policies treating domestic and foreign producers equally that are based on how a product is made (such as bans on goods made with child labor or on products harvested in environmentally destructive ways such as the use of tuna nets that ensnare dolphins). Challenges to domestic laws that implement international commitments, such as Japan's Kyoto Protocol fuel efficiency laws and U.S. laws protecting sea turtles, also must be halted.

2. Undertake An Objective Review of the Uruguay Round. The Seattle Ministerial Declaration must make a commitment to launch an open, objective review of the operations of the Uruguay Round Agreements with broad participation in the design and implementation of the review. The goal must be to identify which aspects of the current agreements need to be amended or eliminated to obtain the broad benefits promised in the Uruguay Round's preamble.

3. Ensure Access to Essential Goods and Services. Food: The basic human right to food security must be kept sovereign. An assessment of the Uruguay Round Agriculture Agreement must focus on food security, especially concerning least developed countries and poor consumers in net food-importing countries. In particular, the impact of large agrochemical and grain-trading multinational corpo-

LORI WALLACH & MICHELLE SFORZA

rations must be examined with an eye toward what international antitrust measures are needed to break up the intense market concentration that now exists. Also, aspects of the TRIPs Agreement must be reviewed with a view toward changing provisions that undermine food security and permit biopiracy. An objective review of the current WTO rules would lead to future negotiations of a food security clause and allow governments to take measures that they deem appropriate to protect food from the effects of conflicting WTO obligations.

Medicines: The TRIPs Agreement must be reviewed with the goal of elevating public health above commercial interests and safeguarding consumer access to essential drugs. The proposals by some developed countries to use the Seattle Ministerial Declaration to push for the expansion of TRIPs Agreement rules are unacceptable.

Services: A review of the General Agreement on Trade in Services (GATS) must consider how the agreement affects the right to universal access to basic services, such as health care, water, education and sanitation, and environmental protection. A review of the agreement also should address the absence of tools to combat monopolistic international mergers and acquisitions.

4. Safeguard Product, Food and Workplace Safety and a Healthy Environment. *Precautionary Principle*: The Seattle Ministerial Declaration must explicitly state, in a manner that binds future WTO dispute panels, that no existing WTO rules shall be interpreted to limit the capacity of governments to establish and maintain nondiscriminatory health, environmental or food safety measures that were enacted based on the Precautionary Principle.

Food Safety and Food Labeling: The Seattle Ministerial Declaration must commit WTO Members to an objective, open review of the Agriculture Agreement focusing on how to modify SPS Agreement rules to enable governments to establish and maintain legitimate nondiscriminatory food safety measures. Such a review must reverse rules relating to burden of proof that now require products to be proven unsafe before they can be regulated or banned. Such a review also must establish a definition of "equivalence" in the SPS Agreement that ensures that foreign regulations provide the same level of health and safety protection as domestic laws and that foreign procedural and review mechanisms are at least as strong as domestic law before they are declared equivalent. The Seattle Ministerial Declaration must clarify that measures to support informed choice by consumers, such as nutritional and informational labeling provisions that treat domestic and imported goods equally (such as GMO labeling), are not inconsistent with SPS or TBT rules.

Product Safety and Environmental Standards: Countries must be allowed to establish their own product and worker safety, health and environmental standards as long as they are not applied in a discriminatory fashion (e.g., France should be permitted to protect its workers from asbestos).

5. Control Merger Mania and Market Concentration. *Anti-Competitive Practices*: Some developed countries have called for the launch at the Seattle Ministerial of negotiations on WTO competition rules. However, no country is calling for the sort of rules needed to deal with anti-competitive business practices and combat the growing threat of monopolistic international mergers and acquisitions. The Seattle Ministerial Declaration should instruct the existing WTO Working Group on Competition Policy to establish mechanisms to:

➤ control anti-competitive and restrictive business practices of transnational corporations (such as price-fixing, transfer pricing and other intra-firm practices); and

➤ review patterns of market concentration and the increasing number of cross-border mergers, acquisitions and alliances.

6. Provide Representation and Redress. *Transparency and Accountability*: The WTO's accountability to the public must be increased in the wake of the Seattle Minister-ial. The Seattle Ministerial Declaration must:

➤ adopt a presumption of openness. All documents of the dispute resolution system (including all party briefs, experts' memos, WTO legal staff memos and rulings) should be de-restricted. Dispute resolution proceedings must be opened to the public;

➤ establish new dispute settlement panel procedures, including: a rewrite of the panelist qualification require-ments to allow for a broader array of expertise; meaning-ful conflict of interest rules; and a guarantee that after the moratorium on environmental and health challenges is lifted, cases raising health, environmental or consumer pro-tection issues shall include panelists with relevant exper-tise; and

➤ tackle the financial, human resource and infrastructure constraints of developing country delegations in a manner chosen by the developing countries to ensure that all coun-tries can participate equally and effectively in negotiations.

7. Ensure Investment Rules Promote Financial Stabil-ity; No Clandestine MAIs. The General Agreement on Trade in Services (GATS), the Agreement on Trade Related Investment Measures (TRIMs) and the 1997 Financial Ser-vices Agreement must be reviewed to consider mechanisms not included in or, in some instances, measures now for-bidden by, WTO rules to ensure market stability. The review should include measures to counter currency spec-ulation and volatile short-term investment (such as the Chilean-style capital controls now being praised by a grow-ing number of international economists).

CONCLUSION

In its short five years of existence, the WTO has had wide-ranging impacts on jobs, wages and livelihoods and on international and domestic environmental, health and food safety protections, as well as on economic development, human rights and global trade and investment. These impacts have not been systematically studied nor have they been well covered in the press. As a consequence, most people around the globe lack an awareness that their lives, livelihoods, food and environment—indeed, their very futures—are being shaped by a powerful new institution.

The WTO is not just about trade and distant economic trends. Rather, it serves as the engine for a comprehensive redesign of international, national and local law, politics, cultures and values. Given how directly and personally this redesign is affecting us all, we hope this pamphlet contributes to public awareness about the WTO and the important choices we face about globalization.

Despite massive public relations efforts to convince us otherwise, there is nothing inevitable about the model of corporate economic globalization by which our world is now being redesigned. Rather, years of planning, lobbying and effort by the few powerful interests who benefit from this model have led to its development and implementation.

There are other models that would result in a more equitable, safe, ecologically sound and democratically accountable society. The question is how the majority of people worldwide who are being ill-served by the status quo can best inform and organize ourselves to make the change.

NOTES

I. THE WTO'S SLOW-MOTION COUP D'ETAT

1   Lloyd Bentsen, "The Uruguay Round—Now," *The Washington Post*, September 13, 1994 at A 21.

2   *Id.*

3   United Nations Development Program (UNDP), *Human Development Report 1999*, Geneva: UNDP (1999) at 3. Also see UNCTAD, *1998 Least Developed Countries Report*: Overview. Geneva: UNCTAD (1998) at 3.

4   UNCTAD, *1997 Trade and Development Report*: Overview Geneva. UNCTAD (1997) at 6.

5   *See* World Bank, *Global Development Finance 1999*, Washington, D.C.: World Bank, pp14-15.

6   Anthony Faiola, "Deep Recession Envelops Latin America," *The Washington Post*, August 5, 1999 at 1.

7   International Labor Organization, "Asian Labor Market Woes Deepening" December 1998.

8   UNDP, *op cit.*, 3.

9   *Id.*

10 U.S. Department of Commerce, International Trade Administration Data.

11 Bentsen, *op cit., n.1.*

12 Brook Larmer, "Brawl over Bananas," *Newsweek*, April 28, 1997at 24.

13 Mike Gallagher and Cameron McWhirter, "Violence and Drugs: Armed Soldier Evict Residents in Chiquita Plan to Eliminate Union," *The Cincinnati Enquirer*, May 3, 1998.

14 This position is reflected in the USTR Statement on the WTO Beef Hormone dispute. USTR, "USTR Barshefsky Committed to Resolving Beef Hormone Dispute," Press Release, Apr. 19, 1999.

15 *See* WTO: Overview of the State-of-Play of WTO Disputes, at www.wto.org/, on file with Public Citizen.

16 *Id.*

17 WTO, *Understanding on Rules and Procedures Governing the Settlement of Disputes* (DSU) at Article 14 and Appendix 3, Paras. 2 and 3.

18 *Id.* at Appendix 3, Para. 3.

19 *Id.* at Article 3.6.

20 *Id.* at Article 8.1.

21 WTO Document WT/ DSB/RC/1 (96-5267), December 11, 1996.

22 Annual Report of Nestle, S.A., Nestle Management Report 1998, Directors and Officers (1999).

23 *Id.* at Appendix 3, Para. 3.

24 WTO, *United States-Import Prohibition of Certain Shrimp and Shrimp Products* (WT/DS58/ AB/R), Report of the Appellate Body, October 12, 1998, *at Para.* 100

25 *Id.* at Article 21.

26 *Id.* at Article 22.2.

27 *Id.*

28 *Id.*

29 *Id.* at Article 22.3.

30 *Id.* at Article 17.3.
31 *Id.* at Article 17.1.

II. THE WTO AND THE ENVIRONMENT

1   WTO, "Trade and the Environment in the WTO," Press Brief, Apr. 16, 1997.
2   Robert Evans, "Green Push Could Damage Trade Body—WTO Chief," *Reuters*, May 15, 1998.
3   WTO, *United States—Standards for Reformulated and Conventional Gasoline* (WT/DS2/R), Report of the Panel, Jan. 29, 1996.
4   *See* WTO, *United States—Standards for Reformulated and Conventional Gasoline* (WT/DS2/AB/R), Report of the Appellate Body, May 20, 1996.
5   62 *Fed. Reg.* 24776, May 6, 1997, at Appendix 19.
6   WTO, *United States—Standards for Reformulated and Conventional Gasoline,* (W/DS2/9), Consolidated Report of the Panel and the Appellate Body, May 20, 1996, at Part C (Conclusions).
7   62 *Fed. Reg.* 24776, May 6, 1997, at Appendix 19.
8   WTO, United States—Standards for Reformulated and Conventional Gasoline, Second Submission of the United States, Aug. 17, 1995, at 22-24.
9   John Malek and Dr. Peter Bowler, *Dolphin Protection in the Tuna Fishery,* Interdisciplinary Minor in Global Sustainability, Seminar, Irvine: University of California Press (1997), at 1.
10 GATT, *United States—Restrictions on Imports of Tuna* (DS21/R), Report of the Panel, Sep. 3, 1991.
11 GATT, United States–Restrictions on Imports of Tuna (DS29/R), Report of the panel, June 1994.
12 "Clinton Pledges Early, Renewed Effort to Pass Tuna-Dolphin Bill," *Inside U.S. Trade,* Oct. 1996.
13 Public Law 93-205, 16 U.S 1531 *et.seq.; see also 52 Fed. Reg.* 24244, Jun. 29, 1987.
14 *Id.* at Article 2.2.
15 *Id.* at Article 2.4.
16 *European Communities-Measures Affecting the Prohibition of Asbestos and Asbestos Products* (LWT/DS 135), Complaint by Canada, May 28, 1998.
17 American Electronics Association, *Legality Under International Trade Law of Draft Directive on Waste from Electrical and Electronic Equipment,* Mar. 1999, prepared by Rod Hunter and Marta Lopez of Hunton & Williams, Brussels, on file with Public Citizen.
18 U.S. Department of State *Demarche* to DG1, DGIII (industry) and DGXI (environment), Jan. 11, 1999, at 4, on file with Public Citizen.
19 *Id.* at Article 4.4.
20 European Union DGXI, *Second Draft Proposal for a Directive on Waste from Electrical and Electronic Equipment,* Jul. 1998.
21 *Id.* at 13.
22 *See* Embassy of Japan. *Backgrounder on Amendments to its Law Concerning Rational Use of Energy Law* (1999), on file with Public Citizen.
23 European Union DGX1, Official Proposal for Directive on WEEE, July 1999.

24 The system employs lean-burn technology that reduces fuel used by means of air intake larger than the theoretical air-fuel mixture ratio, in order to achieve fuel economy. *See id.*

25 Japan, Law Concerning Rational Use of Energy, Jun. 22, 1979, revised Jun. 5, 1998.

26 *See* "TBT Notification 99.003," Letter from European Commission Industrial Secretariat, 1999, on file with Public Citizen.

27 According to Japanese Government sources, the U.S. first weighed in against Japan's fuel efficiency law on behalf of Daimler-Chrysler. At the U.S.-Japan summit in May 1999, Japanese officials reported that the President of Ford Motor Company also complained about the law to the Prime Minister of Japan. Official with Japanese Embassy in Washington, D.C., personal communication with Michelle Sforza, Research Director, Public Citizen's Global Trade Watch, May 13, 1999.

28 *See* Letter from Ferial Ara Saeed, First Secretary of the Economic Section of the U.S. Embassy to Mr. Kazuyoshi Umemoto, Director of the First International Organizations Division of the Economics Affairs Bureau of the Ministry of Foreign Affairs, Mar. 8, 1999.

29 European Economic Council (EEC) Regulation No. 3254/91, Nov. 4, 1991, at Articles 2 and 3, Annex I.

30 Neil Buckly, "New Offer by U.S. on Leg-Hold Traps," *Financial Times*, Dec. 1, 1997.

31 *See* U.S. Trade Representative, *1999 National Trade Estimate Report on Foreign Trade Barriers* (1999), at 115

32 *See* Signatories to Feb. 6, 1996, "Open Letter to Policymakers from Coalition for Truth in Environmental Marketing Information," on file with Public Citizen.

33 WTO Committee on Trade and Environment Document WT/CTE/W/27, "U.S. Proposals Regarding Further Work on Transparency of Eco-Labeling," Mar. 25, 1996.

34 Suggested Basis of U.S. Proposal Regarding Principles Applicable to Eco-labeling Programs, May 22, 1996, on file with Public Citizen.

35 *Id.*

36 "TBT Committee Discusses Labeling, Standards," BRIDGES Weekly Trade News digest, Vol.3, no. 24, June 14, 1999.

37 Keith Koffler, "Administration to Bring Seven Trade Complaints to the WTO," *CongressDaily*, May 3, 1999.

38 (1969) *Vienna Convention on the Law of Treaties* at Article 30(2).

39 North American Free Trade Agreement (NAFTA) at ſ104.

III. THE WTO, FOOD SAFETY STANDARDS AND PUBLIC HEALTH

1 *See* John Canham-Clyne, Patrick Woodall, Victoria Nugent and James Wilson, "Saving Money, Saving Lives: The Documented Benefits of Federal Health and Safety Protections," Public Citizen's *Congress Watch*, Jun. 1995. The authors conclude that over the past 30 years, standards for motor vehicle safety alone has saved at least 250,000 lives and OSHA regulations have saved over 140,000 lives.

2 WTO, *Agreement on Sanitary and Phytosanitary Measures* (SPS Agreement), Preamble at Para. 6: "[T]o further the use of harmonized SPS measures;" *See* also Article 3 on Harmonization.

3 *Id.* at Article 5.

4 *Id.* at Article 5.1.

5 *Id* at Article 3.

6 *Id.* According to a Geneva-based trade official, the Appellate Body move suggests that WTO Members must have conduct a risk assessment before adopting trade-restrictive measures. *See,* "WTO Salmon Ruling Clarifies Conditions For Banning Food Imports, Experts Say," *BNA Daily Report for Executives,* Oct. 28, 1998.

7 *See* European Economic Council Directive 88/146/EEC *cited in European Community Measures Affecting Meat and Meat Products* (WT/D526/ABR), Report of the Appellate Body, Apr. 16, 1998 at 2.

8 "Brie and Hormones," *The Economist,* Jan. 7, 1989, at 22; Samuel S. Epstein, "The Chemical Jungle," *International Journal Health Services* (1990) at 278; A.L. Fisher, et al., "Estrogenic Action of Some DDT Analogues," 81 *Proc. Soc. Expt'l Med.* at 449-441; and W.H. Bulger & D. Kupfer, "Estrogenic Activity of Pesticides and Other Xenobiotics on the Uterus and Male Reproductive Tract," in J.A. Thomas, et al., Eds., *Endocrine Technology* (1985) at 1-33.

9 Among the most vocal critics of the EU ban has been the National Cattlemen's Beef Association (NCBA). After the ban, NCBA president, George Swan, said, "Ten years of false accusations. Ten years of lost markets for U.S. cattlemen and lost opportunities for European consumersË." National Cattlemen's Beef Association, "Government Must Retaliate if EU Continues to Ban American Beef," Press Release, May 10, 1999.

10 *See* WTO, *European Communities—Measures Affecting Meat and Meat Products (Hormones)* (WT/DS26), complaint by the United States.

11 *See* WTO, *European Communities—Measures Affecting Meat and Meat Products (Hormones) (WT/DS26R)*, Report of the Panel, Aug. 8, 1997, at Para. 8.159.

12 WTO Report of the Appellate Body, op. cit n. 7.

13 USTR, "USTR Announces Final Product List in Beef Hormones Dispute," Press Release, Jul. 19, 1999.

14 James Gerstenzang, "U.S. Urges European Union to Avert Toy Restrictions," *Los Angeles Times,* May 28, 1998, at A1.

15 *See* U.S. Department of State, "USG Concerns Over Regulation of Toys Made with Polyvinyl Chloride," *Action Cable,* Dec. 12, 1997 on file with Public Citizen.

16 *Id.* at Paras. 3-5. Denmark, the Netherlands, and Belgium had already instituted voluntary bans on phthalates, PVC-softened toys, or PVC toys.

17 U.S. Department of State Action Cable, op.cit, n. 15, at Para. 2.

18 U.S. Department of State, "U.S. Concerns over Regulation of Toys Made with Polyvinyl Chloride," Action Cable, Dec. 12, 1997, at Para. 15.

19 James Gerstenzang, op.cit, n 14.

20 Stacy Kraver, "Mattel Is Phasing Out Teething-Toy Additive," *The Wall Street Journal,* Sep. 24, 1998.

21 Susan Warren, "Toy Makers Say Bye-Bye to 'Plasticizers,'" *The Wall Street Journal,* Nov. 12, 1998, at B1.

IV. THE WTO'S IMPACT ON EMERGING HEALTH AND ENVIRONMENTAL ISSUES

1   Matthew Stilwell and Brennan Van Dyke, *An Activist's Handbook on Genetically Modified Organisms and the WTO*, Center for International Environmental Law, Washington D.C., Mar. 1999, at 3.

2   WTO, *Agreement on Sanitary and Phytosanitary Measures*, at Article 5.2.

3   WTO, *Agreement on Technical Barriers to Trade*, at Article 2.2.

4   "UN Talks on Genetically Modified Trade Protocol Collapse," *European Chemical News*—CBNB, Mar. 24, 1999.

5   The U.S. is not a party to the Convention on Biological Diversity, so had no vote at the negotiations. However, it was still entitled to participate in the negotiations, and essentially "voted" through the Miami-group initiative. Chee Yoke Ling, "U.S. behind collapse of Cartagena biosafety talks," *Third World Resurgence*, No. 104/105, Apr./May 1999.

6   Andrew Pollack, "U.S. and Allies Block Threat on Genetically Altered Goods," *The New York Times*, Feb. 24, 1999.

7   Chee Yoke Ling, op. cit., n. 5.

8   "EU Accuses US, Others of 'Extreme' Positions That Will Block Biosafety Protocol," *International Environment Reporter*, Feb. 17, 1999, at 136.

9   EEC/90/220, quoted in "E.U. Environment Ministers Strengthen De Facto Ban On GMOs Pending New Law," International Trade Reporter, Volume 16, Number 26, June 30, 1999.

10 *Id.*, at 112.

11 "Member States Reject Application for Two Genetically Modified Cotton Seeds," *International Environment Reporter*, Feb. 17, 1999, at 138.

12 Diane Johnson, "France's Fickle Appetite," *The New York Times*, Aug. 2, 1999.

13 *Inside U.S. Trade*, Vol. 17, No. 18, May 7, 1999 at 28.

V. WTO INTELLECTUAL PROPERTY RIGHTS, ACCESS TO MEDICINES AND PATENTS ON LIFE

1   Stephen W. Scondelmeyer, *Economic Impact of GATT Patent Extension on Currently Marketed Drugs*, PRIME Institute, College of Pharmacy, University of Minnesota, March 1995 at 6.

2   Martha L. Crouch, *How the Terminator Terminates: An Explanation for the Non-Scientist of a Remarkable Patent for Killing Second Generation Seeds of Crop Plants*, Edmunds Institute (1998) at 1.

3   Vandana Shiva, *Biopiracy: The Plunder of Nature and Knowledge*, Boston: South End Press (1997) at 88.

4   WTO, *TRIPs Agreement* at Article 27.3(c).

5   Rural Advancement Foundation International, "Basmati Rice Patent," *Geno-Type*, Apr. 1, 1998.

6   WTO, *TRIPs Agreement* at Article 64.1 .

7   Vandana Shiva, op.cit. n. 3, at 69.

8   John F. Burns, "Tradition in India vs. A Patent in the U.S.," *The New York Times*, Sep. 15, 1995.

9   *Id.*

10 *Id.*

11 *Id.*

12 *Id.*

13 *See*, Thai Network on Biodiversity and Community Rights, "Rationale and Background to the Draft Thai Traditional Medicine and Local Knowledge Protection and Promotion Act as approved in principle by the cabinet on Jul. 15, 1997," on file with Public Citizen.
14 Letter from the U.S. State Department to the Royal Thai Government, Apr. 21, 1997, on file with Public Citizen.
15 Guatemalan Presidential Decree 66-83, Jun. 7, 1988, Article 13: Labeling.
16 Guatemalan Government Agreement No. 841-87, Sep. 30, 1987, Article 12.
17 Frank T. Kelly, Gerber's Vice President for Latin America, Letter to the President of Guatemala, Jun. 16, 1994, on file with Public Citizen.
18 Gerber Letterhead, c. 1994.
19 UNICEF data, *cited in* The Right Reverend Simon Barrington-Ward, "Putting Babies Before Business," *The Progress of Nations* (1997).
20 The Right Reverend Simon Barrington-Ward, op.cit.
21 *Id.*
22 Nutrition League Table, UNICEF, "Protecting Breast-Milk from Unethical Marketing," The Progress of Nations (1997).
23 *Id.*
24 Mario Permuth, Letter to President Bill Clinton, Dec. 12, 1993, on file with Public Citizen. (In the letter, Mario Permuth identifies himself as "the Attorney hired by UNICEF to help support the Guatemalan Ministry of Health.")
25 "Gerber Uses Threat of GATT Sanctions to Gain Exemption from Guatemalan Infant Health Law," *Corporate Crime Reporter*, Vol. 10, No. 14, Apr. 8, 1996.
26 Paul Harris, "South Africa: Drug Industry Threatens to Take S. Africa to WTO," *Reuters*, Sep. 8, 1997.
27 *Id.*
28 Barbarta Larkin, Legislative Assistant to the Secretary of State, Report sent to Rep. Sam Gejdenson (D-CT), House of Representatives Committee on International Relations, February 5, 1999.
29 *Id.*

VI. THE WTO AND DEVELOPING COUNTRIES

1 UNCTAD, *Least Developed Countries Report, 1998: Overview*, Geneva: UNCTAD (1998), at 3.
2 Charkravathi Raghavan, "LDCs to Lose $3 Billion in Uruguay Round," *North-South Development Monitor (SUNS)* 3620, on file with Public Citizen.
3 UNCTAD, *Trade and Development Report*, 1998: Overview, Geneva: UNCTD (1998), at 14-15.
4 Mark Weisbrot, *Globalization: A Primer*, Washington, D.C.: Preamble Center (1999) at 10.
5 *See* "Corporate Profits Year-by-Year," *Associated Press*, Mar. 31, 1999, citing U.S. Department of Commerce, Bureau of Economic Analysis data.
6 United Nations Development Program (UNDP), *Human Development Report 1999*, Geneva: UNDP (1999) at 3.
7 *See* Jane Kennan & Christopher Stevens, *From Lomé to the GSP: Implications for the ACP Losing Lomé Trade Preferences*, Oxford:

Institute of Development Studies, Research Paper for Oxfam Great Britain, Nov. 1997.

8 World Bank, *Global Development Finance 1999*, Washington D.C.: World Bank (1999) pp.14-15.

9 WTO, *Agreement on Agriculture* (AoA) at Part IV. The AoA requires developing countries to remove non-tariff import controls, converting them to tariffs and then eventually removing them.

10 *Id.* at Part V.

11 For example, bananas, coffee, cocoa, beef, veal, sugar and rum.

12 *See* "Vulnerable ACP States," *Lomé 2000*, no. 7, Feb. 1998, at 2.

13 Mike Gallagher & Cameron McWhirter, "Violence and Drugs: Armed Soldiers Evict Residents in Chiquita Plan to Eliminate Union," *The Cincinnati Enquirer*, May 3, 1998.

14 John Tomlinson, MEP (Member of European Parliament), "Going Bananas?" *EU Development Issues*, Autumn 1997, at 1.

15 Brook Larmer "Brawl Over Bananas," *Newsweek*, April 28, 1997 at 24.

16 U.S. Mission to the EU, "WTO Authorizes U.S. to Retaliate in Banana Dispute," Press Release, April 20, 1999.

17 Thomas W. Lippman, "An Appeal for Banana Peace: General Suggests U.S. Trade Fight May Undercut Caribbean Drug Battle," *The Washington Post*, June 6, 1996.

VII. HUMAN AND LABOR RIGHTS UNDER THE WTO

1 George Graham, "Pressure for Social Clause in GATT Deal," *Financial Times*, Mar. 16, 1994.

2 French Decree 96-1133, Dec. 24, 1996, on prohibition of asbestos (J.O. dated Dec. 26, 1996), on file with Public Citizen.

3 Bill Schiller, "Why Canada Pushes Killer Asbestos," *Toronto Star News*, Mar. 20, 1999.

4 *European Communities—Measures Affecting the Prohibition of Abestos Products* (WT/DS135), Complaint by Canada, May 28, 1998.

5 International Organization on Standardization, Standard ISO-7337, 1984.

6 World Health Organization, *World Health Report* 1997, Executive Summary, Geneva (1998).

7 "Burmese leader in exile welcomes limited U.S. sanctions," *Agence France Presse*, Sep. 24, 1996.

8 Act of June 25th, 1996, Chapter 130, 1, 1996, Mass. Acts. 210, codified at Mass. Gen. L. ch. 7. 22G-22M.

9 Prominent USA*Engage members are: AT&T, Boeing, BP, Calix, Chase Manhattan Bank, Coca-Cola, Dow Chemical, Ericsson, GTE Corporation, IBM, Intel, Monsanto, Siemens, and Union Carbide. For a full list, *See* http://usaengage.org/background/members.html, on file with Public Citizen.

VIII. DEMANDS & CONCLUSIONS

1 Guy de Jonquieres, "Network Guerrillas," *Financial Times*, Apr. 30, 1998, at 12.

2 The OECD negotiations on an MAI started in 1995 shortly after completion of the Uruguay Round. Despite attempts by the developed countries to establish comprehensive NAFTA-style investor rights in the WTO, developing country opposition had resulted in a com-

promise on the WTO TRIMs Agreement. The developed countries retreated to their OECD to attempt a backdoor imposition of the NAFTA model worldwide. Until a nearly finished draft text was liberated by NGOs in 1997, neither parliaments nor press in the OECD countries were aware of the MAI. The proposal would have literally empowered foreign investors and corporations to sue directly the any country's federal, state, and local governments for cash damages to compensate for any government action that might undermine their profitability. The MAI talks were forced to a halt by global NGO opposition in late 1998.

LORI WALLACH & MICHELLE SFORZA

AUTHOR BIOGRAPHIES

RALPH NADER
Citizen advocate.

MICHELLE SFORZA
An expert on trade policy and international commercial agreements, Michelle Sforza is the research director at Public Citizen's Global Trade Watch. Sforza has authored numerous reports and analyses, covering such topics as the consequences of NAFTA for the U.S., Mexico and Canada, and the potential impacts of the proposed Multilateral Agreement on Investment. Her articles have appeared in the *Nation*, the *Ecologist*, and the *Multinational Monitor*, among other publications.

LORI M. WALLACH
Lori Wallach is director of Public Citizen's Global Trade Watch. She has been called "Ralph Nader with a sense of humor" in a recent *Wall Street Journal* profile and dubbed "the trade debate's guerrilla warrior" in a *National Journal* profile. Wallach, a trade lawyer, was a founder of the Citizens Trade Campaign, the national coalition of consumer, labor, environmental, family farm, religious and civil rights groups representing over 11 million Americans and also serves on the board of The International Forum on Globalization. She is 35 years old and lives in Washington, D.C., in an old row house she is slowly but surely renovating.

ACTIVIST CONTACTS

**Public Citizen's
Global Trade Watch**
Washington, DC
www. tradewatch.org
202. 546. 4996

**International Forum
on Globalization**
San Francisco, CA
www.ifg.org
415. 771. 3394

**Institute for Agriculture
and Trade Policy**
Minneapolis, MN
www.iatp.org
612. 870. 3405

Third World Network
Penang, Malaysia
www.twnside.org.sg
+60. 4. 226. 6728

50 Years Is Enough
Washington, D.C.
www.50years.org
202. 463. 2265

Alliance for Democracy
Washington, D.C.
www.afdonline.org
202. 244. 0561

People's Global Action
http://www.agp.org

**Center for International
Environmental Law**
Washington, D.C.
www.econet.apc.org/ciel
202. 785. 8700

Friends of the Earth
Washington, D.C.
ww.foe.org
202. 783. 7400

AFL-CIO
Washington, D.C.
www.aflcio.org/front.htm
202. 637. 5000

Women's Edge
Washington, D.C.
www.womensedge.org
202. 884. 8394

**Forest Action Network
Bella Coola, Canada**
http://www.fanweb.org/in
dex.shtml
(250) 799-5800

**Ruckus Society of Art and
Revolution**
http://www.ruckus.org/

Zapatistas
http://www.ezln.org/